To D.J. Willmot

PROFESSIONAL SERVICES
MARKETING
WISDOM

PROFESSIONAL SERVICES
MARKETING
WISDOM

How to **attract**, **influence** and **retain**
clients even if you **hate selling**

RIC WILLMOT

WILEY

First published in 2014 by John Wiley & Sons Australia, Ltd
42 McDougall St, Milton Qld 4064

Office also in Melbourne

Typeset in 12/13.5 Bembo Std Regular

© Ric Willmot 2014

The moral rights of the author have been asserted

National Library of Australia Cataloguing-in-Publication data:

Author:	Willmot, Ric, author.
Title:	Professional Services Marketing Wisdom: How to attract, influence and retain clients even if you hate selling / Ric Willmot.
ISBN:	9780730309994 (pbk.)
	9780730310020 (ebook)
Subjects:	Marketing.
	Sales Management.
	Communication in marketing.
	Success in business.
Dewey Number:	658.81

Cover design by Wiley

Cover image © iStockphoto.com/simon2579

Internal graphics designed by Daria Lacey

Printed in Singapore by C.O.S. Printers Pte Ltd

10 9 8 7 6 5 4 3 2 1

Disclaimer
The material in this publication is of the nature of general comment only, and neither purports nor intends to be advice. Readers should not act on the basis of any matter in this publication without considering (and if appropriate, taking) professional advice with due regard to their own particular circumstances. The author and publisher expressly disclaim all and any liability to any person, whether a purchaser of this publication or not, in respect of anything and of the consequences of anything done or omitted to be done by any such person in reliance, whether whole or partial, upon the whole or any part of the contents of this publication.

Contents

About the author

Ric Willmot assists clients to increase performance and profit by making distinctive, lasting and substantial improvements to their organisations. He partners with his clients to tackle their most difficult issues and serious challenges. Ric is 'The Strategist' assisting organisations to improve performance, profits and productivity.

His work is sought after internationally in improving business growth, success and profits; and he is the go-to person for CEOs, senior executives and professionals practicing in law, accounting, financial services, consulting, recruitment and business coaching. His intent is not just to improve your business, but to build firms which create wisdom and wealth.

Ric typically speaks at over 40 conferences around the world every year; coaches CEOs, executives and business owners to achieve their personal best; facilitates seminars on leadership, power management, change, teamwork, and intellectual development; and delivers guest lectures at universities and business schools on course topics that include advanced management and leadership, entrepreneurship, consulting skills and marketing. Over 230 people from 15 countries have joined his Private Mentoring & Coaching Program and his Members-Only Online Business Forum.

He's interviewed and quoted frequently in the media; writes regular business columns for magazines in Australia, Indonesia, Malaysia, Singapore, UAE and Russia; and is interviewed frequently on ABC Radio and Qantas Airlines Business Radio. His prolific publishing includes more than 250 published articles and 7 books, along with four Learning Modules for the International Institute of Directors and Managers (part of the CEO Institute).

Acknowledgements

I'm indebted to the many clients of Executive Wisdom Consulting Group who over the past decade have allowed me to practise, develop and hone my craft. The work kept me focused on practical results to be achieved in actual client environments. These engagements meant I travelled to countries I would never otherwise have visited, and learned new skills in order to deliver the results they required.

My thanks go to the fine people at Wiley: Sarah Crisp, Keira de Hoog and Alice Berry. Your patience and support went beyond the call of duty and amazingly you chose not to blow me up. To the finest editor I could hope to work with, Jem Bates, who remained calm during the tempest, I thank you for your amazing editing and fabulous support of my writing.

Finally, my eternal gratitude to my family. Especially Dakota, who has waited patiently for Daddy to emerge from his writer's garret and fulfil oft-made promises that sometimes were delayed beyond what a six-year-old would deem acceptable. Your laughter calms the waters, your hugs put the wind in my sails and your love keeps my course bearing true north.

Introduction

You may question why there is a need for another book on business marketing, especially one whose primary audience includes highly successful accountants and lawyers. After all, these are the same people who charge daily fees equivalent to the average weekly wage. (The number of partners of law firms in the United States billing $1150-plus an hour more than doubled to 320 in the first quarter of 2013, up from 158 a year earlier.) However, my experience in consulting to these industry sectors is that people working in professional services are by nature conservative with regard to marketing and selling. That's no surprise when you consider that traditional strategic marketing procedures, by dint of their foundation in advertising or retail, fail to enthuse practitioners in professional services. Therefore, business growth—when it does occur—has more to do with individual efforts of principals and partners (through networking, previous relationships and passive referrals) than with across-the-board implementation by everyone within the practice. Unfortunately, the marketing of professional services is usually a reaction to unexpected opportunities, and nearly always short term. I'm speaking here of such activities as sponsoring events or functions, mass mailing, advertising in professional journals and so on.

Why is this the case? In our complex society most people, especially professionals, haven't the time to cope with all the demands of being in practice, such as administration, employment processes, financial requirements, government regulations, technology updates and continuing education. Owners and partners are required to understand industrial relations, payroll tax obligations, human resources practices, GST and income tax, nondisclosure, and on it goes. All of this and still we haven't yet mentioned actually doing the work for clients. It doesn't seem fair that such a large portion of time is spent on bureaucracy, which produces zero return on investment.

As a professional, you have to assimilate the knowledge needed to be able to help your clients with their issues, problems and decisions, and always be dead honest with them. You will succeed because you become of such tremendous value to your clients that they grow to depend on you. But before this happens, you must first acquire the clients needed to sustain your professional practice. So, you've just added another activity to your long list of things to do: marketing and selling.

Professional Services Marketing Wisdom is a unique and comprehensive marketing blueprint specifically written to take advantage of the Whirlpool Marketing System. The whirlpool requires regular effort to begin. Dipping your toes in the water will basically go unnoticed; you must take the plunge to produce splashy results and get noticed. As you purposely build the momentum of your Whirlpool Marketing, it gains speed and deepens. The centrifugal force creates client attraction at the deeper-level vortex, and the power of your marketing becomes irresistibly strong. Whirlpool Marketing aligns your organisation's overall strategy with daily business development actions. As the momentum builds, the daily marketing activities encircle the day-to-day tasks of the professional's work and efforts. The whirlpool becomes stronger, faster and deeper, feeding its power source from self-fulfilling successes. The astonishing value of Whirlpool Marketing is that at a critical point it becomes more difficult to stop than to maintain and continue.

If you want the whirlpool to work, your activity and efforts that develop the momentum must be consistent and indefatigable. If the movement is not focused in the right direction and completely consistent on the surface, there will be no attraction-force deeper where the income, relationships and return on investment are substantial. If you want the marketing in your practice to succeed, lead from the top and act as an example. A whirlpool is fast—your

Whirlpool Marketing should also be fast. Planning doesn't make action, but only action creates results. Increase the enthusiasm of everyone on staff; create new and exciting service offerings; adapt and embrace any mistakes that could create future successes; abandon what doesn't work (and cannot be successfully adapted); and exploit your current successes further. Do it today, because speed does matter.

Ric Willmot
Brisbane, Queensland
January 2014

CHAPTER I

Identify the clients you want and deserve

Marketing is not only much broader than selling; it is not a specialised activity at all. It encompasses the entire business. It is the whole business seen from the point of view of the final result, that is, from the customer's point of view. Concern and responsibility for marketing must therefore permeate all areas of the enterprise.
Peter Drucker

Professionals will at some point in their career need to win new business. This often occurs soon after the professional has been made partner or starts their own practice. Or it may happen when they have exhausted all available referral opportunities in their networks and friendships. Either way, new business generation plateaus, and possibly even declines, because the professional has never learned how to attract and acquire business. Before you begin to chase after new business you must determine the type of client you really want. Before embarking on any marketing initiatives, first develop a strategy that makes the most sense for you and your business. A poor prospect never makes a great client. A poor marketing strategy will never be compensated for by great marketing tactics, and implementing the very best marketing tactics without a sound and intelligent strategy is akin to prescribing the very best antibiotic for a wrongly diagnosed disease.

In professional services, to be successful you cannot allow yourself to be pigeonholed into a market segment that is not very profitable. And this happens when the strategy is inappropriate or, worse, there is no strategy at all. By developing the most appropriate strategy, you afford yourself a much better opportunity to be the best you can be and develop substantial growth in your firm.

In this chapter you learn:

- to identify the most appropriate market, segments, industries and client types

- to assess the long-term value of a client

- to appreciate the value of a client beyond direct fees

- whether to specialise or generalise

- strategies to sequestrate new business opportunities.

In 2004, at the age of 39, I chose to establish my own consultancy practice without considering that I would be starting from a zero base. No clients, no prospects, and no centres of influence that had a direct connection with organisations that would be in need of the type of consulting I planned to offer. My two previous roles immediately preceding the decision to become a self-employed, independent consultant were as CEO of a human resources firm and CEO of a rugby union football club. The corporate compliance and human resources director of New Hope Coal (who was a contact from the human resources firm) telephoned to ask if I would be interested in helping her with a small project renegotiating employment contracts. Although this was not the field of consulting I was planning for myself, I most certainly needed the work and gladly accepted the opportunity.

The next week I drove 60 kilometres from my home office to the energy company's headquarters at Ipswich to meet with my contact. She explained her objective and why my assistance would be of value to the negotiations; we planned an approach, decided on minimum outcomes and preferred outcomes, and met with the CEO. I cannot say the entire process went to plan because I never had a plan. Sometimes it helps to be lucky. However, there were lessons to be learned from my good fortune:

- My contact saw in me skills and expertise that I had yet to see in myself.

- Many times our professional knowledge transfers to situations that become obvious only in hindsight.

- Buyers decide to engage external expertise because of the results, benefits and outcomes that will be produced for them. They're not interested in your business results or what you have planned for your professional future.

The 'Robin Hood' of professional practices is marketing—it robs the ignorant and gives to the well-informed. Your objective is to identify significant buyers who will profit from your involvement in their business and lives, make yourself available to those buyers and focus on achieving successful outcomes that bring about improvement for them. In achieving these three requirements for your buyer, you in turn satisfy your own requirements.

Your Marketing Whirlpool guides you through the journey of your customer life cycle with your professional practice (see figure 1.1, overleaf). Map the points of business development so that everyone in your practice is aware of your client acquisition process.

- What is the client's point of contact when approaching your practice for the first time?

- What is the entry point for a new client? Or are there multiple points of entry?

- What other steps does your organisation take to nurture the process of on-boarding a new client?

- How does your organisation purposely develop deep relationships with your clients?

Figure 1.1: customer journey and life cycle

Describe the customer journey and life cycle you've mapped for your business.

1 Contact
2 Entry point
3 Nurture process
4 Deep relationship

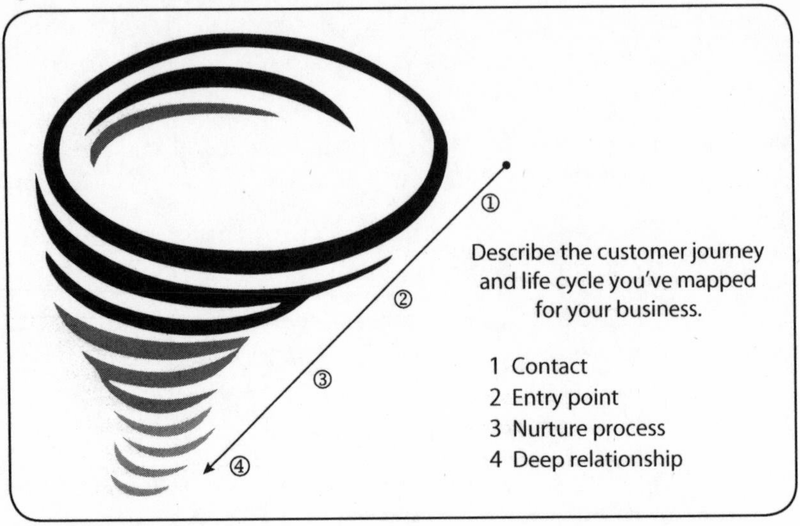

Identify the most appropriate market, segments, industries and client types

On 12 January 2007, *Washington Post* journalist Gene Weingarten enlisted Joshua Bell to perform incognito at L'Enfant Plaza Station of the subway line in Washington, DC as an experiment in context, perception and priorities. For 45 minutes Bell performed on a 1713 Stradivarius violin while about a thousand travellers passed him by on their commute to work. Bell collected $32.17 from a mere 27 people, only seven of whom stopped to listen, and only one of whom recognised him. Weingarten described the crux of the experiment:

> Each passerby had a quick choice to make, one familiar to commuters in any urban area where the occasional street performer is part of the cityscape: Do you stop and listen? Do you hurry past with a blend of guilt and irritation, aware of your cupidity but annoyed by the unbidden demand on your time and your wallet? Do you throw in a buck, just to be polite? Does your decision change if he's really bad? What if he's really good? Do you have time for beauty? Shouldn't you? What's the moral mathematics of the moment?

Even one of the best violinists in the world, playing a $3.5 million Stradivarius, is ignored when he's in the wrong setting. The lesson for us in marketing our professional services is that even if the product or service offering is sensational, no one will buy if the environment is not conducive to the buyer.

Before you accept a new client ask yourself: Will this client and their engagement of your services move you closer to your goals, business and personal, or will they distract you from where you really need to focus? Will this client and their project improve your reputation? Will this client project necessitate that you learn new skills and/or improve your expertise? The environment in which we operate must not only satisfy but enthuse both the client and ourselves.

Whirlpool Wisdom

You cannot create a whirlpool in the mountains. No matter how technically brilliant you might be in your chosen career, if the audience you're pitching to don't want what you've got, you will fail.

Whirlpools do not appear without cause. Neither should you start your Marketing Whirlpool without first establishing the goals and objectives, designing the strategy to achieve them, and only then creating the steps required to generate the motion through force of action.

One conundrum is deciding what types of clients you want to gravitate towards your whirlpool. This is not as easy as it might sound. When I ask, 'Who is your ideal client?' I generally receive one of two responses:

1 'Everyone is a potential client.'

2 Silence coupled with a quizzical look.

It is a question most have difficulty answering. We try so hard not to lose a sale that we fail to do enough to win the right business. Imagine you could have only one client; for your business to be performing at the levels of revenues and profitability you desire, what would that client look like?

Break this down as much as you can and specifically target what it is that makes you genuinely happy with your work.

- What do you do best?

- What type of work exhilarates you?

- What specific client challenges allow you and your expertise to excel?

- When clients refer you, what do they say about you as the reason why you're the person to see?

Your whirlpool activity must attract the clients who will propel you closer to your business goals. The wrong type of client, while fulfilling financial needs, may well steer you to a port you were not seeking. Knowing your ideal client profile enables you to market and brand you and your offerings more intelligently. Knowing your ideal client profile informs you as to whether you are focusing your marketing strategy in the right direction. Marketing your expertise appropriately is more art than science. It's about the art of what's possible, not the science of getting it perfect. There's usually a few equally reasonable ways to achieve successful marketing results. What is imperative, however, is always to ensure that what you are doing is in the client's best interests. If buyers are not responding to your marketing, change something:

- change your offer

- change your target audience

- change your delivery process

- change your price.

If buyers still do not respond, perhaps they just don't like what you're selling.

There is a familiar cliché in Australian business circles: 'Like a car, there is only one way a business can run itself, and that's downhill.' Nothing must be left to chance; there's just too much at stake. Even the sole traders in professional practice will more than likely have the family home mortgaged as collateral against the business. Be clear on how you will become a customer-centric organisation. More on this in chapter 8.

From the Front Lines

'I ran a business breakfast for about 30 clients who had not done business with me in the last two years or more. It cost me $1000—and as a direct result of that breakfast I secured new projects, including a financial health check-up for a client who no longer has their taxes done by me ($3000), a coaching project for two ex-taxation clients who have never responded previously to email marketing for my coaching services ($7500 each), and an in-house training program on how to better use an accounting software package ($2500). About $20K in new business for a $1000 outlay. It's also generated a lot of goodwill.'

—Anita Maclour, CPA

The perils of short-term thinking

'Ric, it's different for you. You're an OD consultant working internationally. All your marketing ideas work for you. But we need to focus on sales activity, not marketing.' Not verbatim, but very close to these words I hear frequently from recruiters, financial planners, business coaches and the like. Building a professional practice on a sales and numbers approach will not create a long-lived, successful business. Managing people by KPIs in areas such as phone calls, appointments, meetings and sales conversions is debilitating and demotivating for your people and negatively affects your corporate brand and repute. 'Sales-based' services firms default to this system because the pressures of an empty pipeline make it so.

Working your business and your people this way can only develop a culture of stress, anxiety and resentment. Therefore, people leave on a regular basis (through their own volition or yours), there's no consistency, and inevitably the doom loop prevails. I think your work as a recruiter, financial adviser, mortgage broker, business coach or consultant is far too important for you to depend on attracting business this way. Utilising Whirlpool Marketing every day will develop a full pipeline, and you and your people get to focus on Key Result Areas instead of Key Performance Indicators.

Build for the long term

- 'It didn't work because we didn't get our article published in that magazine.'

- 'It didn't work because we didn't get to speak at the association breakfast.'

- 'It didn't work because we didn't get that radio interview we wanted.'

There's no strategy or tactic that will work perfectly every time; your sales and numbers approach already confirms that. The magic of Whirlpool Marketing is that your people maintain their self-esteem, your business retains its valued reputation, and your prospects and customers continue their relationships with you; and if you approach the whirlpool process with zeal and enthusiasm — every day — it will keep your pipeline full.

The magic is that you can build on it incrementally; day by day you can grow your Whirlpool Marketing, which allows you to bring the work to the people who want it. Or, you can continue cold-calling and wait for someone who gives in to that type of approach, while your staff casualties continue to make your office look like a departure lounge. Cold-calling is demoralising. Key Performance Indicators are easily managed and recorded, and people can be punished for not making the numbers. Whirlpool Marketing requires effort, time and intelligence, but it's worth doing and builds long-lasting success that makes your business a trusted, relationship-based organisation generating referrals, recommendations and introductions continually.

Ric's Tip

The Whirlpool Marketing tactics and actions that you employ in your firm must be enjoyable. Business is best for everyone in your practice when people are happy and having fun.

Assess the long-term value of a client

The buying decisions of clients are usually based on credibility — your credibility. Proving your credibility is your obligation. It's not enough just to say that you are a competent expert who can best serve your clients. You have to be *perceived* as a competent expert. Before they will engage your practice and your services, your prospective client must believe that you have all of the necessary knowledge, skills and experience to solve their problems or exploit opportunities. This may at first seem unpalatable to you, but you have to appreciate that it is the client who is taking the risk by engaging your practice. For most professional services there can be no guarantee of achieving the desired result. A lawyer cannot guarantee to win a court case. An accountant cannot guarantee a specific dollar amount in a tax refund. A financial planner cannot guarantee an exact investment return. You may feel confident that you can achieve the result required, but you cannot guarantee it, and it is your client who is taking the risk.

If you haven't allayed the fears in the mind of your prospective client regarding your credibility you will find it difficult, if not impossible, to persuade and convince them to engage your professional services. And if you do, you will undoubtedly encounter issues regarding fees and pricing. Throughout this book we're going to reinforce all of the assets you can employ that are constituent marketing and credibility elements.

One of the secrets of Whirlpool Marketing is understanding that there are patterns hidden in long-term customer relationships. There are conscious patterns of communication and there are subconscious patterns that inform behaviour.

- **You have to have rapport.** Rapport is the construct of meeting someone on their own ground — for example, creating your marketing collateral using language that the client would use rather than the language you use internally with your own staff, suppliers and vendors. Most professional services firms speak as if the client has already moved to where the professional is, and then become frustrated because the connection between the professional and the client has not happened. We have to make the effort to reach inside the minds of our target market; to understand their value systems and appreciate what the individual clients seek, want and need. By having an intimate appreciation of what our target customers are seeking we are able to articulate our service offerings, focusing on the results and outcomes the client will achieve by engaging us. You have effectively gone to where they are, understood their needs, and identified the services you provide that will satisfy those needs. That's what rapport is all about.

- **While rapport is necessary, it's not sufficient.** You must also be competent. And it's not enough simply to be competent; you must be perceived by the marketplace as being competent. This increases your credibility. If you don't have credibility in the hearts and minds of your marketplace, they may like you, but they are unlikely to take your advice. Hence, they are unlikely to engage your services. The psychology of purchasers of professional services is that they are unlikely to do something merely because you suggest it's a good idea. They need to believe it best meets their self-interest.

Let's consider the patterns that will help you create credibility in the minds of your target audience. Most of the time, as a professional adviser, you will be engaged to correct a problem rather than achieve a goal.

1   The accountant is asked to reduce taxation liabilities.

2   The lawyer is asked to win a legal action to recover losses, defend a plaintiff's claim or salvage something positive from a bad situation.

3   The financial planner is asked to protect wealth and defer any possible reliance on welfare.

The client says: 'We don't want to put up with this anymore'. The consultant responds: 'Well, what do you want instead?' The trigger is the problem or issue that they don't wish to deal with. Listen to the direction of the language the client uses: does the client want to achieve an outcome, or does the client no longer want to experience the current event?

We generally assume our customers are internally rather than externally influenced, and that they make up their own mind, in their own way, for their own reasons, in their own time. We subscribe to the premise that our customers are motivated to seek out and gather information from what they perceive to be reputable sources and make judgements based on their own internal realities. Customers hold dear standards that inform them about what is appropriate and adequate for them. What we do know for certain is that the decisions of one customer can and will be judged by a different set of benchmarks from the decisions of another customer. Understandably, then, your marketing, advertising and promotional activities do not fall into a one-size-fits-all bucket.

It has to be understood that some customers may be influenced to make decisions externally. That is, their decisions are informed by the standards of others. Some people will not buy a product because another person whom they respect stated that they would never buy that product. Some buyers will choose between two competing products because another person whom they respect stated that product A was superior to product B. When customers go external (to someone or to a situation), meeting the client where they are will certainly not be sufficient to influence them to choose the buying decision you would like them to, because they take their cues from others.

Appreciate that the hardest clients to influence are those with an internal pattern. Consider teenagers. When parents tell them to turn off their computer game and tidy their room, what happens? Nothing. When a peer tells them they have to download the latest YouTube video or meet them at the local shopping mall, what happens then? Teenagers have internal patterns with their parents and external patterns with their friends. The context differentiates the pattern.

Your clients have the potential to behave, and process decisions, using similar contexts:

- internal with professional advisers

- external with friends and peers.

Determine the value of a client beyond direct fees

If I asked you to rate how important marketing is to you and your organisation on a scale of 1–10, you would no doubt answer '10'. If I then asked you how competent and astute you personally were at marketing, your answer would be lower. Much lower in some cases. Many confuse old-school 'selling' with intelligent, respectful marketing, and therefore shy away from the implementation or try to outsource it to staff or external contractors. Lawyers and accountants, in the main, are especially shy of marketing and mostly avoid the activity, all the while impressing upon their staff its importance. Stop attempting to persuade the client to buy what you're selling. Rather, identify their key objectives, needs and wants, assess the solutions that they seek, and then determine how you're able to provide those solutions that will best satisfy their needs. Clients are impressed by being helped, not being sold. The value of any client is not in the initial sale, but in the longevity of the relationship.

A common mistake made by professional services providers is to measure the value of a client by the amount of fees received from that client. But clients have much value over and above direct fees. Think beyond the immediate sales opportunity and consider how you can develop a long-lasting relationship with the client. How can you be of such immense value that they are thinking of how they might use you next? This is a far better business development proposition than thinking how you might make your next sale to the next client. Some clients may in and of themselves not generate substantial revenues; however, they can refer and recommend you to many more people who fit your preferred client profile. You would agree this constitutes a high-value client regardless of the direct fees received.

Most independent professionals do not think past the current client project. They're so consumed with what's 'on the table' that they are deaf to the cues of future leverage, in all its guises. Being technically brilliant and competently skilled in your profession as an accountant, lawyer, financial planner, business consultant, recruiter or business coach does not guarantee a constant stream of high-paying clients, let alone a high income. Taking a long-term view of any new business relationship, coupled with an intelligent process of reaching out laterally from existing clients, can earn you two, three or ten times the average income of the self-employed professional without this perspective.

Graduates of my mentoring and coaching program explain that what was most exciting for them was to learn to think of the fifth, sixth and seventh sale when engaging for the first time with a new client. Adopting this philosophy guarantees that the initial marketing results are never one-hit wonders. Instead, the results consistently repeat themselves as the Whirlpool Marketing system uses strategies that are not events, but a way of behaving every day in your business life.

Decide whether to specialise or generalise

Not everyone needs to be a specialist. In the medical profession, significant numbers of general practitioners make a very good income through a practice that would be the envy of many. It's as admirable to be a generalist in professional and personal services as it is to follow a path of specialisation in your field. Not everyone needs to be a forensic accountant or an intellectual property rights lawyer. Balancing the argument is the recognition that the world is becoming ever more complicated, in spite of the claims that technology is making our lives easier. The increased burden of our complicated lives has created opportunity for the well-informed. It's impossible, or at least difficult, in professional services to be all things to all people.

A key to your success as a professional services adviser is your decision on whether to make the transition from generalist to specialist. By examining your existing clients you can analyse their characteristics to determine if there is an identifying uniqueness evident in the demographics. Your decision is made easier by answering these questions:

- Specifically, what type of work do you do most?

- Is this work profitable, and significantly so?

- Is this work more profitable than the other services you provide?

- Is this work enjoyable and satisfying to you and your team?

- Do you like working with the types of clients who need these specific services?

- Do you perceive a significant market for this type of work that you have the capacity to reach?

- Is the demand for this type of work likely to continue for a significant period?

Simply choosing to become a specialist does not in itself guarantee significantly higher fee levels, revenues or profitability. If you do identify a niche market that is in severe need of a specialisation that you are competent to deliver, you will be wise to seriously consider the opportunity that brings.

When your business becomes known as a specialist you can afford additional time to become the master of your domain. By specialising, you are privileged to maintain your current and ongoing education in a narrow field, which means you become even more expert at that specialisation, thereby remaining at the cutting-edge of professional advice in your specific area. It certainly would be a difficult ask for a generalist to be at the leading edge of competency and expertise across all of the services offered. There is no reason for a specialist to cease offering the full range of services that a generalist might. For instance, the larger law firms have partners practising in their own individual areas of specialisation, while the organisation through all of its professional staff is able to provide any service that may be required by any client at any time.

Perception also influences people's buying decisions. If someone believes — rightly or wrongly — that their problem or circumstances are unique and require the attention of a specialist, they are unlikely to engage the services of somebody who is considered a generalist. This is not to say that the buyer is correct or that a generalist couldn't do an exceptionally good job. But the reality is that what the client perceives is all that matters when choosing a professional to solve their problem. Specialisation and fee levels are intrinsically linked, as the client perceives that the specialist has a more expert knowledge in a very narrow area. Buyers who have a need of this expertise are expecting and willing to pay a premium for that knowledge.

Being a generalist means that you will more likely be selling in a horizontal market and limiting your geographic reach. Horizontal markets usually relate back to median fee levels and commoditised thinking, which is not a bad approach if the market is large and can sustain numerous competitors. However, as a generalist your fee level is a dominant factor in the decision-making process of your prospective clients. Being a specialist means that you will be selling in a vertical market, and geography and price become less influential in buying decisions. Vertical markets, while mostly unrestrained by geography, have fewer people and organisations in need of their services.

There is always a risk with specialising too narrowly. You must be confident that any vertical markets you address have appropriate capacity and potential to supply the levels of business you require to both sustain and grow your practice. What may appear to be lucrative specialties in vertical markets might be dangerously thin offerings in the long term. There is also the potential geographic disadvantage of vertical markets that require more travel than would normally be expected in providing your service.

You Can't Make This Up

Business relationships and customer service are degrading at a rate that would give the most seasoned of astronauts vertigo. Here's what I have personally experienced or been witness to. All these events are 100 per cent true. As Bart Simpson says, 'You just can't make this stuff up!'

- Failing to return phone calls. Everyone wants referrals, and yet people foolishly believe they don't need to display common courtesy. If customers stop doing business with your organisation, *you* will soon be out of a job. Customer service is *everyone's* job, no matter what title they have printed on their business card.

- Staff at a Starbucks in Singapore allowing a woman to hold up the line for 7 minutes while she decided what type of coffee she would order.

- Not delivering on promises. The editor of an Australian business magazine has been promising for three months to send me the PDF copies of a few articles I wrote for his magazine. No sign of them. I did, however, receive an email asking me to refer him potential advertisers.

- Just minutes prior to a confirmed 11.30 am meeting, I receive an email stating the prospect was home sick and couldn't meet with me.

These people are like black holes, imploding, increasingly immersed in their own world, and in their acts of self-absorption they also trap us in the debris.

On the upside, the funniest comment I received was at a coffee meeting with a CEO client where her HR manager said that after seeing my photo at the top of my website, she thought I would be taller. I'm 5' 11".

Strategies for isolating new targets of opportunity

Do you wonder why marketing for professionals is such a challenge? Much time is wasted on marketing done sporadically, independently and tactically, without the framework of an intelligent strategy. If you believe that being a competent professional is marketing enough for your practice, consider the *Tyrannosaurus rex*, the most ferocious carnivore in the history of alfresco dining, who despite all its might and power became just as extinct as its prey. Being technically good is no longer enough to grow a professional practice. You must be continually isolating new targets of opportunity to sustain your pipeline.

- Is there a particular issue that is uppermost in the consciousness of a specific group of clients for which you have high-level competency and expertise? Being able to address a current and most relevant topic of concern to a specialised group of prospects allows you to be seen as the go-to person for them.

- Do you have connections within your network who can recommend you to business groups, trade associations, business schools and universities, and the like? Being recommended to senior executives at these organisations gives you a substantive advantage over competitors coming in cold.

- Who are the people you know who can arrange for you to meet face-to-face with key decision makers working in the organisations that for you would be highly prized clients? We tend to underestimate the reach of people within our existing networks, so we fail to ask enough questions of the right people who could give us key card access to the executive suites.

- Do you have a long history of working within an industry sector where your depth of experience affords you status as an elder statesman? Having a broad and deep knowledge of an industry provides you with an understanding of the nuances that makes you of particular worth to that group. The incisive knowledge you have gained allows you to parachute into any organisation within that industry and be seen as one of the team.

- Are you able to quote CEOs and/or senior executives who can validate the quality of your work in their industry? Approaching Coca-Cola suggesting your expertise to assist with equipment refinancing, and having a testimonial praising your skills from the national purchasing manager of Pepsi, is a strong starting point.

- Can you present or speak at an event aimed specifically at a target industry you are hoping to infiltrate? Are you able to have your intellectual property published in a magazine representing that target industry? Speaking at an event or having your work published in the industry magazine, which exposes you to key decision makers, catapults you immediately to expert status. You're viewed as an industry expert and buyers will seek you out.

- What networking events can you attend where the buyers in your target industry will be present? Meeting and conversing at casual gatherings is a pleasant way to break the ice and personally introduce you to key buyers. When you follow up by asking for a formal meeting, those buyers who have met you will be more approachable and amenable to granting your request. Being in business and not networking is like winking at a girl in the dark. Nobody knows what you're doing but you.

At the commencement (top) of your Marketing Whirlpool (see figure 1.2), the ease of interaction with prospective clients encourages them to begin penetrating the market. Here you focus on your no-cost and low-cost offerings to the market. At this level, you are in a competitive space. The deeper you delve into the interaction with clients, and the deeper their penetration into the market, the more distinctive your marketing offerings should be. Your brand and reputation are influencing buying decisions. As you reach deeper again, your marketing offerings become more sophisticated, the price points for client purchase rise. Your client relationships are now at their strongest, and their investment in you at its greatest. You have moved from simple interactions and no-cost offerings (newsletter or blog subscriptions, for example) at level 1, through incremental steps that see the client investing significantly to gain access to your most sophisticated and valuable expertise at level 13.

Figure 1.2: customer journey and whirlpool penetration

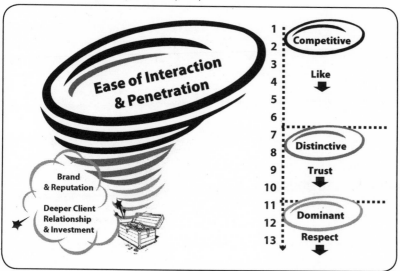

Keep your eye on the landscape and be ready for opportunities in propinquity. Opportunity is not a single event but in motion all around us. We just don't always recognise what's on offer. This isn't to say that you take a scattergun approach to attacking new targets of opportunity. Far better to be a sniper and pick off the opportunities one by one with accuracy and intensity. Isolating the targets of opportunity is about recognising quality not quantity.

Best Practices

What are you measuring? If you're a lawyer, you need to be continually opening more files because that means you're doing more business. If you're an accountant, you need to be getting new clients or doing new work with existing clients because that means you're doing new business. No matter what your profession, it's all about revenues, clients and profits. That requires marketing and selling. So, are you making sales or are you measuring activity? Just because you make 50 calls to see 20 people, then send five proposals, doesn't mean you've been profitable. The catchphrase 'It's all in the numbers' is ludicrous. There's a big difference between activity for its own sake and productivity and profit.

Measure what matters:

- Is this the best use of my time?

- Is this activity producing profits?

- Is this activity getting me in front of true economic buyers instead of feasibility buyers?

- Is this activity getting me referred to other quality prospects?

- Is there a better activity that would produce higher quality results?

In promoting your expertise, your best advantage over the competition is to understand the client. Stop selling and start helping. Usually you will uncover the truth from your clients by asking probing and provocative questions, and not accepting the first answer provided. Behind every logical 'want' there will also be an emotional 'need'. You will be most successful in marketing your expertise and services when you manage to help people with both. Why are they seeking to do this right now? What created the need? Is something broken and needing to be repaired, or is the client seeking to improve upon what they are already doing? Understanding your clients affords you the credibility to boldly promote why you're the best choice of all the professionals available.

CHAPTER 2

Why you're the best choice for your market niche

Price is what you pay. Value is what you get.
Warren Buffett

When you have identified the most appropriate client–demographic to support your business strategy, you need to ascertain your market niche. Why is this important? Because it determines your fee levels. Your niche is governed by the type of service you provide and where you provide it. You'll increase revenues by expanding your geographical reach, finding additional niches and/or providing additional services to an existing niche. Dominating your niche and keeping the competition at bay is the ultimate goal.

In this chapter you learn how to:

• know when it's time to expand

• offer new services to existing clients without losing credibility

• maximise your fees working within your niche

• increase fees using 29 proven techniques

• create an agile advantage.

When you have identified the most appropriate client demographic to support your business strategy, you need to ascertain your market niche. Why is this important? It determines your fee levels. Your niche is governed by the type of service you provide, and where you provide it. You can increase revenues by expanding your geographical reach, finding additional markets, and/or providing additional services to an existing market. Dominating your niche, keeping the competition at bay and being paid appropriately for your expert services are your ultimate goals. Competition rarely puts anyone out of business — they usually put themselves out of business by arrogance, stupidity, poor quality or ignorance of what's obvious around them. Make good choices and your competition will seem far less threatening.

While a component of Whirlpool Marketing is to churn the waters and create waves, being busy for the sake of it will not produce splashy results. The centrifugal force of your whirlpool must capture the attention of your ideal clients. Attracting a school of sardines when you're fishing for tuna isn't being successful. Fishermen chum for sharks — that is, they fertilise the waters with enough entrée to entice the big fish to come looking for the main course. Although the analogy is crude, the point is sound. By freely sharing useful information that benefits prospective clients, you will encourage them to come looking for more.

A caveat: Intelligence is a significant factor in the whirlpool's success. This isn't a process where 'any old thing will do'. Your marketing must be smart, concise, incisive and valuable...as perceived by the client.

There are various reasons why professionals decide on a market niche they wish to infiltrate. But do the assets of the professional practice, and those who sail in her, represent a positive fit for that market niche? An analysis of the central competencies and core beliefs of your organisation can steer you towards a destination port that best accommodates your ship.

- What do we do exceptionally well that proves us to be better than most competitors in our marketplace? What area of our performance receives the clients' five-star rating and stamp of approval?

- What do our A-class clients say about our work and us? What were they looking for that was their key criterion for selecting us? What are the primary objectives, outcomes and results that they want and we can give them?

- Is there anything in the methodologies of our business approach that aids us in delivering exceptional value for our clients?

- How is our firm fundamentally different from the competitors in our marketplace? What innovative services do we provide? What do we do that other professional practices do not?

- Where is the exclusivity that clients are willing to pay extra for?

- What is the one facet of our business that we are most known for, and that gets talked about the most by our clients? If we could deliver only one specific professional service, what would it be, and how much would it be worth to our clients?

- Is there anything distinguishable about the way we think, as an organisation, that draws clients and business to us?

- In what areas do we have specialised knowledge and skills for which our clients hold us in high regard?

- What is it that we are not?

> *If you are not prepared to resign or be fired for what you believe in, you are not a worker, let alone a professional. You are a slave.*
> **—Howard Gardner**

Know when it's time to expand

Business is full of tough decisions. The economy can be volatile and it's not always easy to know what the right decision is for you. One misstep can hurt a business and create problems that take a long time to overcome. You do have indicators that can help, however. The decision to expand a business is triggered by positive trends, increased revenues and sales, and positive economic forecasts by the media. The expansion can be as big as creating a second location, or as small as creating a few new positions or adding a service.

An indicator that you may be ready to expand some parts of your practice is there's no more capacity within the firm for you to delegate because your people are already at competent capacity. Or, as I outline in chapter 11, you may be better advised to take a contrarian view and, rather than expand, increase your pricing. Leaving that point aside for later discussion, you must decide if it is in your best interest to expand your service offerings (see figure 2.1). Your first consideration will be to determine whether a new service offering would detract from your core business. Making the wrong decision can be a costly mistake. Alternatively, it could be that the trigger allows you to gain a competitive advantage over your competition and develop new profit centres from your existing clientele.

Figure 2.1: services offered

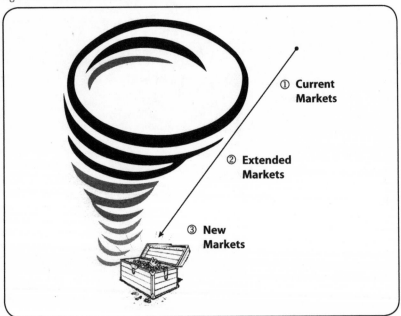

Questions to consider when making decisions regarding the expansion of your services and products include:

- Will you be required to employ additional staff with new skill sets? If so, how much will this cost you?

- Will your existing staff require additional training and development? If so, at what cost to you in terms of money and productivity lost (non-billable hours) for your staff?

- How much demand have you been able to quantify from your existing clients for this new offering?

- What is the financial potential of offering this new service (pessimistic, realistic and optimistic)?

- Has an assessment been made of the cost in time for staff diverted from core business activities to this new service offering? Does the return on the new service offering exceed the loss to your core business activities?

- What is the risk to the practice, the staff and your reputation if the venture fails?

- What is your gut telling you?

Focus on the client's needs and wants. Just because you love what you do technically, it doesn't mean that your clients care one iota. If you want to be the service provider of choice for your preferred clients, you must show them why you're the best choice—for their reasons, not for yours. Your industry awards may be gratifying to you and your spouse at the black tie dinner where you receive your trophy, but the client cares only about what you've done for them lately. I'm not discounting industry awards completely. Special recognition, excellence awards, certifications and the like help build your credibility, which is valuable. There may be clients who will be persuaded to consider you in your practice based upon such accolades. You will find being the recipient of any such awards and accolades has immense value for publicity and media promotion. For this reason as well, registering and nominating for such 'trophies' is a worthwhile activity. However, I emphasise that your clients care about *their* business results, not yours.

You Can't Make This Up

'Hello Ric, Jeff from Sydney here. Trevor said you could help me. I've had a great business for 10 years but the current economic climate has really knocked us around. How can we get through this?'

What's different from before?

'Clients are cutting back on recruitment costs, new job orders have almost stopped and the ones we do get are arguing about our fees. It's murder out there.'

What's your business?

'We offer specialist recruitment services where we do psychometric testing of all applicants, then we fully research...' He went on with much more of the same but I've no idea what he said. I had to interrupt.

You try to find applicants for your client's job vacancies?

'Well, we're different from most other recruitment firms... but that's essentially it.'

How are you fundamentally different?

'Like I said, we do psychometric...' Life's too short. I interrupted, again.

There are lots of fine recruitment firms delivering all of those services and value-adds. And Jeff, if it takes you as long to explain your value-offering to prospective clients as you took to me, you're losing their attention fairly quickly.

Lesson learned: we must articulate how we provide value and a return on investment for clients. Why else would they want to engage us? No matter what our profession.

1   What are the three most important reasons people are buying (and should continue to buy) from you?

2   How will your clients measure the ROI you provide for them? And how can you show this to them so your offer is so compelling they must invest in you right now?

3   Is your communication style clear and concise?

We develop a business model that allows us some favours over time. Being seen as one of the tribe is one example. When you've done good work within a niche for some time, and your clients have become advocates of your work, you can reach a point where you're 'one of us' and you get an all-access backstage pass. Seasoned journalists have become adept at this strategy, gaining privilege not afforded rookie reporters.

Offer new services to existing clients without losing credibility

The value of your current customers can last a lifetime, but the truth is your current customers can be much more profitable than you think. The American Institute of CPAs estimates that attracting a new client is eleven times more costly than keeping an existing one. By investing in existing customer relationships, you are essentially increasing the effectiveness of your marketing and advertising by a factor of eleven. This is why focusing on your existing customers, and determining how you may be of increased value to them by providing additional services, is a worthwhile strategy for your practice. Granted, it is a fine line you walk as a professional adviser, and it is imperative that whatever recommendations you offer your clients are for their benefit, not yours. Presenting suggestions for existing clients to engage you for additional work is always done for the purposes of improving the client's results and outcomes. This is not manipulation. Manipulation is in the motivation, and your motivation is to advise your existing clients on how they can be even more successful or achieve even greater results. Your clients will appreciate you for being proactive and your credibility is maintained because you have ethically considered the client's interest first.

The more value you have provided for your clients in the past, the greater trust and respect they have for you, and the stronger your relationship is with them. Therefore, when you identify a need or an opportunity of which your client can take advantage, they will more readily accept your advice and act upon your suggestion. At this deep level of relationship price is no longer a consideration, so long as it is reasonable and appropriate compared with the return on investment the client will receive for implementing your advice. It's imperative that you keep in mind the principle behind Whirlpool Marketing: your objective is to attract customers, not to sell them. Presenting strategies and ideas that will benefit your clients, and explaining in a relaxed, low-key way how and why the strategies and ideas are good for them, is appreciated by the client, especially when you provide options of how they may move forward with the suggestions. That's not selling—that's being of immense value.

- What problem is my client currently experiencing that is hampering their success?

- What opportunity for improvement or growth is available to my client of which they are not yet taking advantage?

- What could my client implement into their business today that would help them be even more successful than they already are?

Identify opportunities to expand and grow business revenues by selling extended products and services to your existing markets, and then by selling completely new products and services to your existing markets (see figure 2.2).

Figure 2.2: markets served

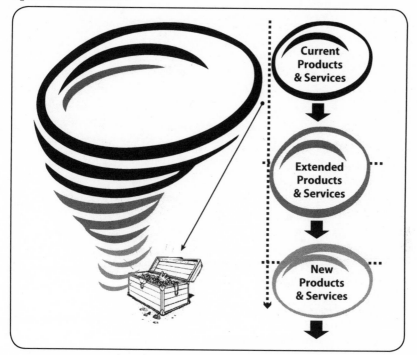

From the Front Lines

'We have found that in our practice those customers who really trust and enjoy our advice and service are more likely to refer us. Word-of-mouth can be one of the best ways to develop new customers and when those referrals come to us from existing clients who accept our recommendations without questioning our prices, nearly always those people accept and trust us in the same way. Those are wonderful clients to deal with and we're always delighted to receive more like them.'

—Andrew Cohen CPA

Maximise your fees working within your niche

People new to their profession are inclined to make mistakes with the pricing of their services. One mistake I witness regularly is keeping your fees low until... until you have more experience; until you have that next certification or designation; until you have 50 clients on the books (or 100, or 200). A New Zealand accountant joined my mentoring program at the top-shelf level on the recommendation of her friend and lawyer. During lunch in Auckland, we outlined five key objectives over the next six months. One was pricing strategy. 'Ric, I'm hesitant to raise my fees too much until I have 500 clients on the books.' I was concerned about how she might ever find the time to eat lunch again. When do you say, 'That's enough'? My best advice to you is, there's no better time than now. If you're serious about engaging with your clients and giving them your best, then you need to relieve yourself of any anxiety and worry. During the pre-flight safety demonstration, the flight crew direct you to secure your own oxygen mask before attempting to help children or others. You cannot help anyone until you first help yourself. You are much more 'present' with your clients when you're under less stress.

Rolls-Royce, Bentley and Ferrari don't discount even when the economy is tough and the competition is fierce. They appreciate their own value and market only to the people who will appreciate that value. The right clients will pay a premium if they believe they can achieve faster, better or more permanent results. Aldi supermarkets are clear about who their buyers are, and they are not the shoppers who demand high-quality products and a multitude of choices. Aldi has successfully created a business model that markets to a narrow niche, producing volume and obsessively focusing on keeping operating costs low. To sustain low prices Aldi offers only one or two options of any given product. In this manner, the stores can operate in premises with smaller footprints than other supermarkets that carry more choices. This translates to lower rents in major shopping centres where the square meterage leasing rates are exorbitant. Aldi know their market, and they've purposely chosen a business model that focuses on volume and low pricing. What choice do you want to make your professional practice? Do you want to be the Aldi of accountants, or would you prefer to be the Rolls-Royce model? If you choose the latter then your quality has to be *el primo*.

The combination of extending your services offered (see figure 2.1, p. 24) and your markets served (see figure 2.2, p. 29) maximises the business potential of your practice (see figure 2.3).

Figure 2.3: merging markets

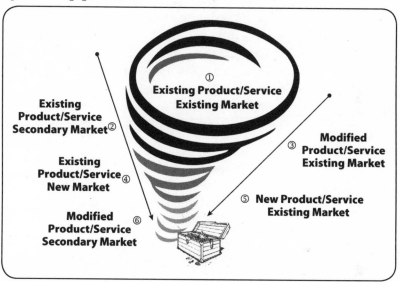

Existing Product/Service
Secondary Market②

① Existing Product/Service
Existing Market

③ Modified Product/Service
Existing Market

Existing Product/Service④
New Market

⑤ New Product/Service
Existing Market

Modified ⑥
Product/Service
Secondary Market

Whirlpool Wisdom

Not every point in tennis is won with an overhead smash. Subtlety can be the match-winning play. When prospective clients ask you how much you cost—before you've reached positive agreement about what needs to be done—you shouldn't answer directly. How can you? You don't know for certain yet what the client needs. When a prospective client enquires about how much other work you've done in their industry, focus on the issues the prospective client is facing and explain how you've successfully assisted multiple clients in many industries with similar issues.

Increase fees using 29 proven techniques

Not everything that counts can be counted and not everything that can be counted counts.
—**Albert Einstein**

I have been championing value-based pricing strategies since I started my own tax practice in 1987, and one of the most frustrating aspects of teaching professionals about pricing is the tendency to generalise the conclusion that the clients won't like it. Granted, clients may need to be re-educated to accept value-based pricing and the merits of such an approach—for them. So, how might you more intelligently price your professional services and increase your fees? Here are 29 proven techniques to charge what you're worth and have your clients gladly pay you for that value.

Awareness

1   Ensure your clients are fully aware of the complete range of your services and offerings. Don't assume they know all of what you do. Don't presuppose that you cannot learn something new and add to your toolkit.

2   Think of the long-term relationship you can create with a new client, rather than solely the first sale and the money currently on the table. Your objective is to nurture clients to ultimately ask your advice about everything-business, even when they know you don't do that type of work. You know you've developed a strong bond with a client when they call you and say something like, 'I know you don't do this, but who could you recommend I speak with?' Now you know that the client has assimilated with you and depends on your advice and guidance. You will never miss an opportunity with this client, so long as you don't fall asleep in the crow's nest.

New clients have yet to make a deep investment in you. There's no guarantee that this isn't your first and only project with them. As you build the relationship and the momentum of your Marketing Whirlpool with them, the projects become more frequent and the client learns to trust you. You reach the chest of treasures when your Whirlpool Marketing has built such a deep relationship that the client uses you in preference to other service providers, depends on you and hence has assimilated with you (see figure 2.4).

Figure 2.4: depth of partnership

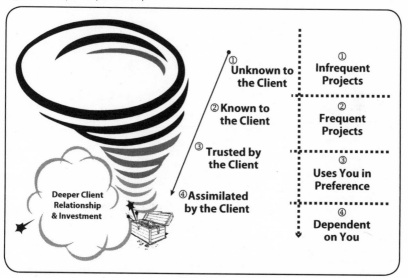

3   Always ask the prospect what they're attempting to achieve. Keep probing and never assume the first answer is the accurate, complete or only answer.

4   Always provide options for the client to choose 'how' to engage you. Giving them a take–it–or–leave–it proposal increases the risk of them leaving it ... and leaving you for your competition.

5   Always provide an option of exceptional value to the client above the stated/assumed budget. It's arrogant of any professional to assume what the client is willing to invest to improve their business. Before meeting you, the client wasn't aware of how much better her organisation could be and the results that could be produced.

Figure 2.5 shows an example of an accounting firm's whirlpool of service offerings. As the offerings move deeper (with the provision of more in-depth services and advice), so does the client commitment (with deeper levels of financial investment and respect for the accountant), as shown in table 2.1.

Table 2.1: the deepening of client commitment

Service offering	Fee range	Whirlpool attraction	
Compliance Bookkeeping Accounts preparation BAS & IAS Audit Tax returns FBT, GST, CGT Superannuation Company returns Corporate secretarial BAS audit protection	\$1000—\$5000 per annum	COMPETITIVE	LIKE
Business advisory Business Health Check Cash-flow management Management reporting Budget preparation Tax planning advice Self-managed super funds Benchmarking Valuations and appraisals Business financing Salary-packaging Selling businesses	\$5000—\$25 000 per annum	DISTINCTIVE	TRUST
Business improvement Strategic planning Business plans Business consulting Business coaching Financial planning Property services Risk management Wealth strategies Estate planning	\$25 000 + per annum	DOMINANT	RESPECT

Figure 2.5: an accounting firm's whirlpool of service offerings

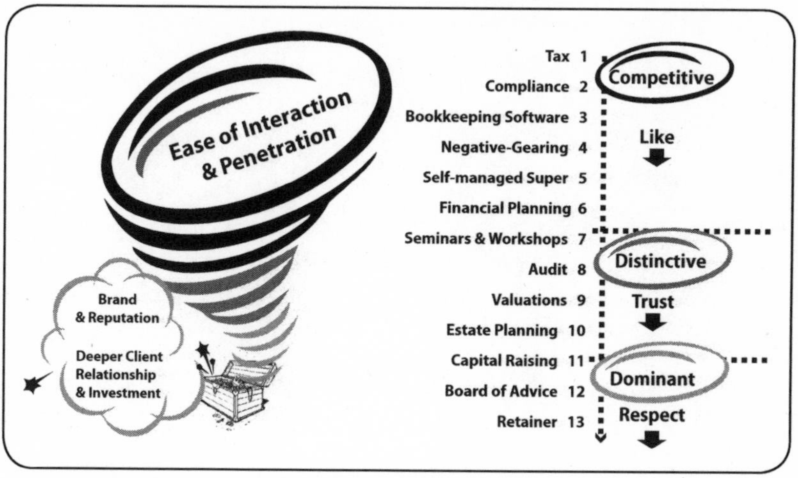

Confidence

6   Always be prepared to decline bad business or bad clients. If you perceive that this client or project could get difficult or, worse, nasty, don't go there. Better to pass it up and use the free time to market for your ideal clients and projects.

7   Never accept unethical, illegal or immoral business.

8   State and explain your fees with clarity and dignity. Do not hesitate.

Professional assistance

9   Look for ways to improve, grow and develop the client's organisation, not solely to fix problems. The builder is worth more than the repairman.

10   Be proactive (assertive) rather than only reactive (passive).

11   Any employees who are salaried professionals on staff should be given a budget for generating new business revenues and acquiring new clients for the firm.

Engagement

12   Move beyond solely what the client wants and ascertain what the client needs.

13   Have the client participate in the diagnosis—don't prescribe independently of the client.

14   Establish the value of your engagement in concert with the client. Have the client help you determine the complete value of improvement in their business through your intervention.

15   Never pay bribes to win business, no matter what country it's in. It's globally unethical.

Price

16   Do not base your fees on what your peers are doing. It's an all-too-common mistake, especially when leading business schools and coaching companies are giving that very advice. Why imitate a peer who is possibly getting it very wrong?

17   Base your fees on the value (monetary and intrinsic) received by the client rather than the task you perform, or the time you invest. Never utilise time measurements of your performance as the determination of your value to the client. Conversely, if the client needs you to achieve milestones, outcomes or results in quick time, you become more valuable, hence your fee is increased.

18   Stop thinking about what the client can afford. If the prospective client cannot or will not accept your fees, and you must reduce the client's investment in you, there must be a reduction in value and/or a quid pro quo from the buyer. This must be established and agreed to before finalising the contract agreement to engage your services.

Agreement to proceed

19   If they agree to pay your full fee in advance, right here, right now, you can provide a modest discount to win the business.

20   If there are components within the scope of the project that you cannot do, subcontract and retain control of the entire project. Do not allow the project to be split and compartmentalised. You could potentially lose control of not only the project but also the client.

Receipts

21   Offer incentives for payment in advance and 100 per cent payments in full.

22   Never agree to fee write-offs after work has been completed.

23   Never accept payment for your professional services based upon contingency.

Ongoing relationship

24   If a project is separated into bundles, chunks or phases, offer partial rebates to guarantee and capture the future business, thereby protecting the future project components from a competitor. The competitor may well be the client, who could choose to do future components (promised to you) internally.

25   Introduce and offer new value to your existing clients to increase business with those accounts.

26   Do not accept referral business on the same terms as the referent. For many reasons, such as longevity of business and size of revenues, you may be providing preferential pricing, terms and/or conditions to an existing client (the referent). New clients referred to you by the referent do not qualify for the same preferential treatment ... yet.

27 Prepare your client in advance for giving you referrals—
    internally and externally. Referrals to other buyers
    within an organisation are just as valuable as referrals to
    other organisations.

Nuances of buyer's psychology

28 If the buyer asks about your fees prior to establishing goals
    and objectives, agreeing on the objective and subjective
    measures, and determining the tangible and intangible
    value from the successful outcome of the project, decline
    to answer. Explain that you cannot possibly know, because
    until you have reached conceptual agreement you cannot
    ascertain what you'll be required to do. Imagine your car
    won't start. You call the dealer and immediately ask how
    much it will cost to fix. The dealer knows your car won't
    start but can have no idea what repairs will be required to
    fix the problem.

29 If you 'wrote the book', the buyer will attribute greater
    value to your advice and expertise. Examples of people
    who have increased their professional fees after authoring
    successful books include Russell Ackoff (problem solving),
    Ron Baker (value pricing); Robert Cialdini (influence and
    persuasion), Seth Godin (permission marketing), Marshall
    Goldsmith (executive coaching), John Kotter (change
    management) and Peter Senge (systems thinking). You
    don't necessarily need to write a commercially published
    book, but it will be helpful if your intellectual property is
    disseminated in print and via the internet in the form of
    opinion pieces, position papers, research papers, case studies
    and the like.

Best Practices

There are occasions when discounting your fees makes perfect sense and is entirely appropriate. As an example: a discount for volume work. Be certain, however, that you maintain control over this dynamic. Allow the discount only at the tail end of the work. By enacting your discounting procedures in this manner, if the client needs to cancel any of the work included in calculating the discount, you're protected.

For instance: You have a Standard Service Offering that you price at $2500 per project. A client requests 10 of these projects over the next six months and asks you to consider providing a discount. You're willing to provide a 15 per cent discount because the work is standardised, your practice has capacity to handle the workload of the 10 projects without burden, and they're implemented over a relatively short period of time. You provide the client with two options:

1   The client pays the full amount upfront and receives a 15 per cent discount (10 × $2500 = $25 000 less 15 per cent discount ~ the client pays you $21 250 in advance of commencing the first of 10 projects).

2   The client pays for each project and a 12 per cent discount is apportioned over the projects on a sliding scale (see table 2.2).

Table 2.2: project discount on sliding scale

Project	Standard fee	Payment required
1	$2 500	$2 500
2	$2 500	$2 500
3	$2 500	$2 500
4	$2 500	$2 500
5	$2 500	$2 500
6	$2 500	$2 250
7	$2 500	$2 250
8	$2 500	$2 000
9	$2 500	$1 750
10	$2 500	$1 250
		$22 000.00

Ric's Tip

In Thailand, while I was on a change management consulting assignment for a petroleum company, a handwritten message on a chalkboard outside a hairdressing salon caught my attention as an astute example of taking what would be generally considered a 'commoditised service' and positioning it as a value offering. It read:

'Sorry, we don't do cheap haircuts, but we do fix them.'

Create an agile advantage

Most businesses seek to differentiate themselves from their competitors and express an advantage in terms of benefit to the buyer. A considerable investment of time, money and resources is made on this very objective. And many small businesses have a distinct advantage that they not only shy away from but invest time, money and resources in denying its very existence within their organisation. *Being agile.* Small business has the inherent ability to respond quickly, to adapt to change rapidly as and when needed, and to remain nimble. This is a considerable advantage over larger, more cumbersome competitors. But many attempt to create the illusion that they are in league with the big boys, pretending to be anything but an agile small business. Clients are best served with speed of response and swift solutions. The big end of town has more resources, but small businesses have the agile advantage. Resist surrendering your agility, continue to behave in an entrepreneurial manner, and be swift to capitalise on opportunities before the corporates can manage to assemble their troops. Are you in the moment with agility and speed, or are you burdened by tasks and bureaucracy?

Speed matters. Initially use small experiments. If these experiments deliver little to no results, immediately cease. Where the results achieved are at least moderate, dive deeper into the whirlpool, concentrating your momentum on what works. Start small, move quickly, learn quickly. It pays to be agile. At this point there is no need for a fixed budget. There is a great need for complete flexibility. Setting short-term milestones allows you, your people and your organisation to celebrate the achievements and then set new milestones rapidly. This will lead to deeper impact and greater flexibility.

When you hire new staff for your practice, are you hiring these individuals because they bring additional skill sets to the firm? At every opportunity, you should be broadening and strengthening the knowledge and expertise of your organisation through your employment practices. This creates powerful agility in your firm by adding disparate and diverse skill sets that allow you to respond to all opportunities that present themselves. If every time you hire a new staff member you merely replace what is lost through the exit of another employee, or replicate what you already have, you have in no way improved your practice. Promote the benefits of being agile to your target audience in the form of business outcomes:

- 'Our firm provides superb value for money because we're not burdened by large overheads and infrastructure costs that have to be added in to our fees.'

- 'You never get passed down to interns. Our approach in working with you is: it's personal.'

- 'We're immediately responsive because we're small and agile.'

- 'It's in your interests to achieve quick solutions. By maintaining our agile size, we guarantee speed of results.'

Show your clients the ROI in having you on board. Explain what is fundamentally different about what you can offer because of your agile advantage. It doesn't have to be unique (there's nothing new under the sun), but it does have to set you apart from your direct and closest competitors in the mind of your client. Perhaps it's how you deliver the business results. Or the way your methodologies and processes make more sense with regard to the client's best interests. If you don't tell people about your agile advantage, they probably won't know about it.

The business of professional services is a moving beast, but never before has there been such a transformation for some professions. The most radical changes are happening in accounting, financial planning and law. As an example, the accounting profession is increasingly competitive and if you're not diversifying and aggressively marketing, you're at a distinct disadvantage. There is no 'typical' accounting practice model that will guarantee or prevent success. However, essentially those leading and setting the strategy of the practice, must be cognisant of where and how the profession is changing.

Brent Szalay, Managing Director of Seiva Accountants & Advisers in Melbourne, Australia is clear that the business of compliance (tax returns) has no long-lasting future and that accountants necessarily must become genuine consulting partners with their business clients.

'Capturing important business information from the client allows us to document the back office processes and integrate the client's systems into cloud-based systems like Xero. By doing this we can provide real-time feedback and advice to our clients where we're focusing on reducing the costs of doing business rather than simply completing tax returns. The 'back office' has become the new point of focus, and the innovative developments in technology allows us to automate this and facilitate the client's business technology to 'talk' to our financial technology culminating in the automation of information analysis. Quality information is the linchpin.'

Seiva is an accounting practice that has set a strategy to go far and beyond the normal accounting advice. The Whirlpool philosophy informs all of us in professional services to extend our existing work, adapt what we're currently offering, and create new ways of working with clients that we've never done before. Whether you're in accounting, financial, HR, consulting, or law, you must continually find avenues to become even more valuable than you already are. It's wise to identify what your clients need, and show them you have the solution. Resonate, differentiate and substantiate.

CHAPTER 3

Establish thought leadership and attract true buyers

If your actions inspire others to dream more, learn more, do more and become more, you are a leader.
John Quincy Adams

Thought leadership is key not only for acquiring clients but also for attracting higher fee levels for your services than might otherwise be possible. If you do not blow your own horn there is no music. Thought leadership is a subtle but highly effective way to have your horn tooted for you through endorsements and substantiation. This allows prospective clients to perceive your credibility and feel comfortable in paying you a premium for your services.

In this chapter you learn:

- what thought leadership is and how it directly affects your fee levels

- the tangible and intangible value of the client testimonial

- how the right publicity can establish you as an expert in your field

- when writing articles is appropriate and how to do it easily and well

- how to identify your past 'hidden' activities to help develop your credibility.

Genuine and legitimate thought leadership is a valuable instrument that contributes to the success of any professional services firm. Those contributions include:

- guarantee a positive and influential point of differentiation between you and your competitors

- demonstrate your ideas, opinions and insights into the problems, challenges and issues prospective clients consider important and relevant to them

- provide your target audience with a sample of your expertise, whetting their appetite for more and giving them the impetus to seek you out

- exalt you as a critical thinker and a leader in your field

- offer the opportunity for candid conversations with prospective clients about the wants and needs they have and the problems that are serious and must be addressed

- are generally less expensive than advertising, with significantly better results

- attract and acquire new clients. Thought leadership holds a prominent position in Whirlpool Marketing because it attracts quality buyers. It creates a gravitas that pulls potential buyers into your whirlpool, and these tend to be buyers who seek expertise and respect value.

Thought leadership campaigns are an effective way to commence that dialogue because you engage prospects at their point of need, when they are most approachable and accepting of helpful ideas. Most traditional marketing tactics are premised on a 'push' approach. Advertising, direct mail, trade shows, seminars and telemarketing push your brand and service offerings to those who don't yet know about you (or, at least, don't know you well). The expectation is that at some time in the near future they'll require your expertise, remember you and reach out. The mistake is to utilise such awareness tactics but then fail to offer anything of value to prospects drawn by the promotional activity. While these have their place in a sound annual marketing plan, they are incomplete without a 'pull' strategy.

Pull marketing is predicated on a different notion: giving away value to those in need at the instant they most need it. Pull marketing doesn't tell the market what you do; it exemplifies how, by using your strategies, a prospect can solve a problem they care about deeply. One way to demonstrate that you can solve such problems is to write case studies and position papers. Publishing case studies and position papers, either in print or on your website/blog, is a positive and powerful way to explain your expertise and the results you can achieve for clients. A well-written case study should promise real-life solutions and offer insider tips that can be immediately implemented by the reader. Short case studies fashioned as marketing vehicles are surprisingly effective.

Best Practices

In business, any task is made easier by finding or creating a process to guide you through to completion. The same holds true for writing case studies. It is a process that can be refined and replicated.

1   Organise your information under major headings:
    a. challenge or issue
    b. approach or solution
    c. result or current situation.

2   Reveal the business pain that needs to be solved.

3   Include specific, quantifiable results—you can include data relating to the situation before and after the solution is enacted. Many times a 'before and after' comparison table for data is an excellent way to exemplify your expertise and the results created.

4   Build suspense—just like any good read, the case study is more interesting if it takes the reader on a short journey and incorporates emotional anticipation.

5   Include a conclusion that not only satisfies the reader but has them excited about what might be possible for their business.

One concern professional advisers have is that describing exactly how you would solve a problem is akin to giving away the farm. Perhaps. In May 2000 my wife and I purchased a beautiful

Queenslander in inner Brisbane to renovate. But even after reading all the DIY books, I still call local tradesmen to do the job properly. Just because someone tells me how to build a house extension, it doesn't make me a carpenter. When you explain how to approach and potentially solve a problem, you're giving an insight that perhaps prospective clients didn't have before, and this encourages them to consider more carefully the expertise available. If your prospects and clients have the capacity and competency to solve their problems themselves, they would already have done so. You have nothing to lose by sharing your intellectual property.

What thought leadership is and how it directly affects your fee levels

Ric's Tip

You can recognise a thought leader—they are the people cited by others to prove their points of view.

Let's first be clear about what thought leadership is not. It is not just white papers. It is not a thinly disguised sales pitch about what you do. It is not webinars that talk about your latest service release or customer success story. Thought leadership tells your target-profile decision makers exactly how to solve a problem they really care about. The elegance of this marketing tactic is that it opens doors to decision makers, causes people to be attracted to you, and primes them to speak with you about issues you can solve. The prospect comes to you pre-qualified as a genuinely interested buyer, aware and educated about your style of approach, and often seriously motivated to discuss engaging your professional services.

When book reviews are written and published, sales increase. Transparency improves quality, which improves sales, which improves profits. The more transparent you can be in business, the more profits you are likely to make. When customers see transparency as being the norm rather than the exception, their purchasing decisions are influenced by quality. Customers for whom quality is a purchasing criterion are more willing to pay for that quality. Disseminating your thought leadership freely into the public domain, where your target audience will be exposed to it, heightens the opportunity for people to engage you. When clients approach you, price is not the first thing they'll discuss. They have approached you because the exposure they have had to your thought leadership has legitimised a decision in their minds that you're the best person to help them. Fees are not the primary concern in this conversation. The more of an expert you are perceived as being, the more willing clients are to pay you appropriately for your quality of knowledge and advice.

You will fast-track the appeal and attraction of your practice by disseminating your knowledge through various media. The more knowledge you share with the marketplace, the more you will dominate and differentiate your practice, thereby securing the option to increase your fees commensurate with the increase in your value (see figure 3.1). As your practice matures you significantly increase your access to knowledge.

Figure 3.1: knowledge domination

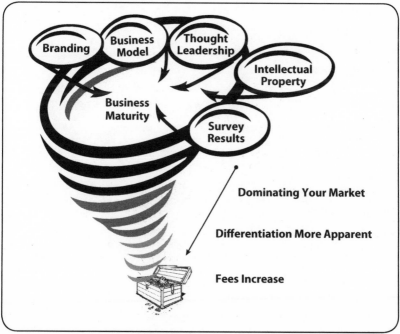

The tangible and intangible value of the client testimonial

The best business is repeat, recommended or referred; of that there is no doubt. The instrument of choice to build that type of business is the 'testimonial' from clients you have worked with who are enthusiastic and supportive of the good work and service you provide. The challenge is how to request and receive quality testimonials. The best time to seek a testimonial is while you are still engaged with the client on a project or contract, or 'sale'. Many gurus advocate writing the testimonial yourself and emailing it to the client to have them transfer it to their own letterhead and sign it. This makes it easier for the client.

That may work, but some might view it as mendacious. Better to have the client write the testimonial in their own words so when these commendations are used they definitely do have meaning, virtue, varied tones and diverse messages.

- Make the request for a testimonial part of your business process as you are confirming the sale, contract or engagement. By letting your client know very early in the relationship that you'll be asking for this favour, it prepares them positively for when you do ask for it.

- Include copies of other testimonials you have already received to confirm that your client is in good company and to provide some guidance. Isn't this approach better than writing it yourself?

- Request the testimonial about two-thirds of the way through the project. You have greater potential for success when you are still engaged and physically interacting with the client than after the work is completed and you have, like Elvis, left the building.

Whirlpool Wisdom

Start with your best and biggest customer and identify the reason why they choose to work with you. Take that reason and articulate it in a way that is unique to you and can be protected from replication by your closest competitors. Develop collateral to support its value and then market it to your largest potential audience. Make it yours—own it, defend it and promote it unashamedly.

How the right publicity can establish you as an expert in your field

Is it possible to demonstrate thought leadership when what you are doing as a professional practitioner is exactly what your competitors are doing? My experience, after more than a decade of consulting to varying professional practices around the world, indicates that most firms are not doing exactly what their competitors do, and that, counterintuitively, being unique is not as important to your clients as is your level of expertise, competency, customer service and previous client engagements. Clients are more respectful of your deep-level understanding of the key issues they are facing. Thought leadership is your opportunity to show how your practice has that level of understanding of key issues and that you are the best people to solve the client's problems associated with those issues. This opens doors that your competitors may not even know exist.

Thought leadership marketing, perfectly positioned, will be more effective than most traditional marketing campaigns at generating new business leads. Consider the advertising you have used in the past. How much new business can you definitely track back to that advertising? How many telephone calls or emails did your practice receive because of that advertising? The limitation of advertising is that it is impossible for people who are exposed to the message to have a clear understanding of the problems your practice can solve for them. Consider the cost of an advertising campaign; advertising of any type is never cheap. Alternatively, what makes thought leadership incredibly attractive as a marketing instrument is its cost effectiveness. The cost of a one-off, full-page advertisement in a trade publication or an association magazine will be a minimum of $3000 to $5000. A full campaign throughout a series of magazines and newspapers could range anywhere from $100 000 all the way up to $250 000. With numbers like this the intelligence and efficacy of thought leadership as a key pillar of your marketing activities begins to make incredible financial sense.

When writing articles is appropriate, and how to do it easily and well

Communications such as e-newsletters and blogs that were once thought revolutionary now seem somewhat commonplace. Everyone from my bank manager to the real estate agent to the neighbourhood handyman produces a newsletter, a blog and free articles. Even value-based fees—which I was utilising in my own tax practice in 1986 and have been advising and coaching others on ever since—no longer seem revolutionary, even if most professionals still do not embrace the strategy. But no matter how much is published, well-written, thought-provoking, relevant articles will always attract the attention of discerning readers and prospective clients.

Producing quality, high-value content is a way to differentiate your business, but as the noise increases it becomes more difficult to be heard. What is the emerging medium or method to keep prospects interested when confronted with an ever-increasing barrage of content—some valuable, some not? If you are already the marque of your industry, that's fine, but how do you get noticed when you're an unknown and unproven commodity? You need to have three personal traits:

- strength

- passion

- fearlessness.

You must be willing to stand out in a crowd. Expertise, authority and recognition reach above the noise. In fact, that's why they call the rest 'noise'. You should focus, as a top priority, on creating above-the-noise repute. You must make waves. Forging a new piece of intellectual property, or creating a powerful product, or perfecting the sales language you need to use — that's not noise, that's a message that matters. Writing for publications, both online and offline, can be a potent and cost-effective marketing tool. It requires only one good idea — seen at the right time — to motivate a potential client to call and ask for your help. Most professionals, though, don't do what's necessary to become published. This is disappointing because there are many with brilliant minds who have so much to share. Consider, if you will, consulting and advisory services: all these firms strive to be recognised as thought leaders and attempt to utilise that position as a pivotal component of their marketing and branding. Given that consulting and advisory practices are in the business of 'ideas', none of this comes as a surprise nor is it likely to change soon.

But you don't just start writing, imagining that editors and publishers will fall over themselves to print your stories. Article writing for the purpose of being published will generate some visibility and hopefully offer potential leads to new business relationships. Create a publishing whirlpool to facilitate a better chance of success.

- Who do you want to read your articles?

- What publications do those people read?

- What associations and business groups do those people belong to?

- Do those associations and business groups have their own publications?

- Do those publications accept unsolicited submissions?

- Is there a theme, layout or style that the publication appears to adhere to?

- Are you able to provide a submission that fits with the publication's style and would be of genuine interest to their readers?

The reward for being published in a business magazine is not so much who reads the article in the magazine. The benefit to you as a professional services adviser is to have the magazine publish you and your intellectual property. You request a PDF of the article as it appears in the publication so you are able to send that article to the specific prospective clients whom you want to read it. Sending a prospective client your intellectual property published in a recognised trade journal, association organ or business magazine has significantly more cachet than sending exactly the same words printed on your letterhead. It is your responsibility as part of your Whirlpool Marketing to ensure prospective clients whom you wish to attract receive this collateral.

From the Front Lines

The Law Firm Marketing Masters podcast rated me one of the 'Top 10 Law Firm Marketing Experts in the World' and 'Australia's leading law firm management and marketing expert' in 2012. This doesn't just happen—you make it happen by following the Whirlpool Marketing System. Develop thought leadership, disseminate intellectual property and consistently introduce value into your market space. It doesn't matter if you're an accountant, lawyer, recruiter, financial planner, consultant, coach, professional speaker...the rules are the same.

A proven process for writing

To write your thought leadership pieces (an article, for example), a simple but effective approach can save enormous time. This is just one technique for getting ideas out of your head and onto the page.

1   Choose the audience you seek to influence—readers who fit your value proposition (5 minutes). [Financial planners]

2   Choose a topic that will be provocative, or vexing, or controversial, or captivating, and timely. (10 minutes). [Transitioning from commission to professional fees]

3   Choose a working title (5 minutes). [Fee Only Financial Planning: How you can make the transition]

4   Select 3–7 key points (10 minutes). [1. The mistaken thinking on fees; 2. How to establish a purposeful pricing model; 3. How to transition existing clients; 4. The key to managing client relationships when they have to pay for your services.]

5   Write an avant-garde, gritty opening paragraph (10 minutes). ['Why do clients care less about the amount of commission and so much about a fee that is comparable or less than what would have been deducted from their original investment? If the objective is to increase their wealth, then we should first decrease what is being usurped from the investment capital. That's not usually done with front-end commissions.']

6   Write about each of your points, making sure to include your rationale, an example so it's not merely conceptual and a graphic if it helps explain the point (20 minutes per point).

7   Write a closing with a call to action (10 minutes). ['The next time prospective investment clients walk into your office, invite them to sit in a comfortable chair, offer them some refreshments, and remind yourself that you represent their best opportunity for creating the maximum wealth for their future financial security. Ask yourself how they might speak positively of the experience, because you are a fee-based planner. That alone might increase your business more than you can imagine.']

8   Reassess the title to see if you want to change it (5 minutes). [How to Charge What You're Worth: And have your clients gladly pay you for that value]

This entire eight-point process requires about two hours. Spread it over four days, and it's a half-hour a day. Diarise it in your calendar at 9.30 each morning—and don't change it, no matter what.

You Can't Make This Up

In my first year as a self-employed independent consultant, I decided that publishing articles in business magazines would assist greatly in developing brand recognition around my name. One magazine focused on SMEs and was publishing articles written by professional speakers whose names I recognised from the National Speakers Association Australia. It did appear to me, however, that these were advertorials as every article was associated with an advertisement somewhere in the magazine. The magazine published its advertising rates—the cost was $3000 for a full page. I wrote three articles of varying word counts in a style similar to others in the magazine. I posted the articles with a note to the managing editor stating that if at any time the magazine was left with white space as they neared the deadline to go to print, they would be welcome and authorised to cash my enclosed cheque for $200 and publish one of my articles. Over the next three editions of that magazine all of my articles were published, and the cheque was never cashed.

Think differently

The concept of thought leadership has been attracting marketers since 1994 when Joel Kurtzman, editor-in-chief of the magazine *Strategy + Business*, coined the term to designate people who had contributed new thoughts to business. When done effectively, thought leadership leads to market leadership. Content that conveys actionable insights will cut through the communications clutter of everyday life and connect with customers in a way that adds value. It is the content of these messages that sets the firm apart. You need to take some pretty bold positions on some issues, offering a different perspective from the conventional wisdom handed out every day like pamphlets on the street corner, to establish your credibility as a thought leader.

Taking advantage of the benefits thought leadership has to offer does not necessarily mean the thought leadership has to be embedded only in your professional practice. Joe Kafrouni, the principal of Kafrouni Lawyers, displayed a wonderful example of 'reverse thinking'. Joe wanted to deliver an extraordinary value-add to 25 of his A-class clients in a gesture of thanks for their continuing trust in him. He contacted me and asked if I would be willing to present a half-day workshop to his 25 clients sharing my thought leadership of how they could improve their businesses. In a masterstroke of selfless modesty, Joe exposed his clients to a thought leader from a different profession. The benefit to his clients was that they gained access to new information that was immediately implementable in their businesses. The benefit to Joe is that his top 25 clients are now grateful for his generosity in providing them with the opportunity to learn something new that would otherwise have cost them thousands of dollars to access.

Implementing articles as part of your Whirlpool Marketing will reap benefits for your professional practice only if you make a commitment to being regularly published. Presupposing that you can write well, a few published articles will perhaps generate some brand noise, and provide you with PDFs for reprinting and dissemination to targeted prospects. This alone, however, will not guarantee your being seen as a thought leader or independently attract the attention of the audience you seek. Article writing and being published must remain one of the ever-present core tactics of your Whirlpool Marketing. Except for a lucky few, most of us will not become overnight stars and be sought out for our ideas and opinions by magazine editors. You may well consider that your intellectual property is disappearing into the business media vacuum, but remain patient because it requires repeated exposure to capitalise and produce business results for your professional practice from publishing. The effort involved is more than worthwhile because the return on investment is potentially enormous.

Dive deeper than simply publishing

Many professionals assume the total worth of an article is in its being published. Wrong! The process of writing is an opportunity to meet prospective clients, explaining your network of contacts, and strengthen existing customer relationships. This is achieved by inviting clients, prospects, colleagues and peers to provide quotes and information for the articles you write. This way you are providing multiple perspectives on any given issue, your reputation is enhanced by being in good company, your article may be seen as more credible because of the input of others, and you have the opportunity to interact with these people and strengthen your relationships with them.

Publishing articles is one small piece in the jigsaw of a commercially successful business and just one of a multitude of activities in the Marketing Whirlpool that you use to generate interest in you within your marketplace. Nothing happens until you sell something, and you have to be selling continually in order to generate business income. The questions you need to ask yourself are: 'Where do my A-class clients reside? What is it that is causing them the most pain at the moment? Do I have a palatable solution to that pain? Of those who have the pain and would be willing to accept my solution, which of them have the propensity to invest money in buying that solution from me?' Get yourself in front of these buyers frequently enough with quality intellectual property so that they reach out to you and ask your help. Convert your article into a tool that gets you in front of true buyers with a genuine need for your services.

Thought leadership is akin to recruiting a salesperson to sell you, your firm and your services. If you were to read the job description for this salesperson it would include:

- available to work anytime, night or day, 365 days per year

- has no requirement for time off for public holidays, sick leave or annual leave

- has an acute ability to unerringly recite the same story thousands of times; is willing to educate, entertain and enlighten the prospect while also working towards the sale; and is always focused on the client

- cooperates well with all other marketing initiatives within the business

- works for free.

Identify your past 'hidden' activities to help develop your credibility further

It will happen that sometimes you're so busy that focusing your attention on writing articles, case studies and the like is difficult. So much so that even coming up with ideas on what to write about proves impossible. Generating ideas for article topics need not be a tribulation that eats away actual time. You can stimulate your creativity by addressing a series of questions:

1   What is different or unusual about your target audience?

2   What is different or unusual about the features of your services?

3   What is different or unusual about your key clients?

4   What is different or unusual about the problems facing your clients?

5   What is different or unusual about the challenges your clients have in implementing solutions?

6   What is different or unusual about the results some of your clients have achieved that were not completely expected?

7   What is different or unusual about your understanding of...?

8   What is different or unusual about your knowledge of...?

9   What is different or unusual about the speed of results some of your clients have been able to achieve by implementing your solutions?

10   What is different or unusual about your technology?

11   What is different or unusual about your problem–solving techniques?

12   What is different or unusual about your analysis and research of client issues?

These 12 targeted questions most assuredly have the potential to stimulate your thinking around what your target audience would most like to read about.

The Thought Leadership Whirlpool (see figure 3.2) takes your prospective clients on a journey from first being exposed to your intellectual capital through to enquiring about how you might help them.

Figure 3.2: thought leadership

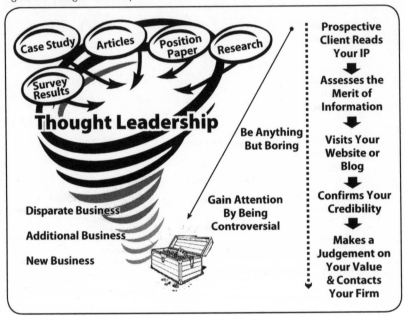

Put all your thought leadership activities together to create greater credibility

You can never be published in too many magazines or newspapers. With over 200 articles published in hard copy magazines in 17 countries, my personal brand and market reach enables me to expand my business globally. It's not easy and you'll be rejected. You need discipline, consistency and tenacity.

You can spend weeks researching, writing and editing your white paper, case study or article expecting that prospective clients will clamour to download it from your website or blog. It will not make a difference to your business results or make the process worth the effort if that is all you do. You must market the white paper, aggressively, through your whirlpool. To make your piece of thought leadership marketable, it has to be visually appealing. Use graphics, colour and high-quality paper if printing. The purpose is to get it in the hands of people who can engage your services, so make it readily accessible through a multitude of channels:

- Post it on your website and blog.

- Offer it to other bloggers.

- Offer it to appropriate associations and business groups.

- Send an email to the specific contacts on your database for whom the thought leadership piece is relevant.

- Send it out in a direct mail campaign to customers and prospects; if you have a regular e-newsletter, promote it in your next regular mailing or include it in a permanent callout box on your e-newsletter template.

- Offer it to alliance partners and colleagues.

- Send a media release to the relevant publications, radio and television.

- Consider engaging the services of a public relations firm.

- Use it as a 'leave behind' on sales calls.

- Consider creating podcasts, webinars and brief articles from this content.

Thought leadership is something I could write an entire book about, and perhaps Wiley's Acquisitions Editor might send a contract soon requesting I do just that! But for the purposes of this book you've been provided with enough information to attack the concept and the process of being an exceptional thought leader within your profession. Veterans and neophytes alike can utilise a multitude of approaches and various thought leadership methodologies to acquire new sources of business. I have explored only a few of my personal favourites here. Be mindful that it's always better to create a topic that applies your specific expertise to the current concerns of your clients, rather than calling upon your general knowledge to address generic problems.

1   Choose the audience you seek to influence.

2   Choose a topic that will be provocative (or vexing, or controversial, or captivating) and timely.

3   Choose a working title.

4   Select 3–7 key points.

5   Write an avant-garde, gritty opening paragraph.

6   Write about each of your points, making sure to include your rationale, an example so it's not merely conceptual, and a graphic if it helps explain the point.

7   Write a closing with a call to action.

8   Reassess the title to see if you want to change it.

Contrary to what might be expected, article writing—done well—is not a common phenomenon in professional services. Articles shouldn't take long to write. Some people procrastinate for days or weeks over completing an article and others never finish, protesting they're not an author. An average article targeted for publication by a business or professional magazine will usually be in the range of 400 to 1000 words. After practice and the right approach, this will require only about 30 to 90 minutes. Using the following straightforward approach, you can easily modify for length by adding or deleting 'points of wisdom', 'examples', 'data', 'evidence', 'metaphors' and so on. As you become more comfortable, conversant and competent with my format, the writing will require less time, you'll experience less apprehension and stress, and you'll accept more opportunities to be published, thereby becoming a prolific writer.

1   Select the single most important client (or prospective client) you would like to read your article.

2   Write for that person as if they were your only reader.

3   Provide pithy, straightforward, pragmatic ideas, advice and strategies rather than obscure abstractions.

4   Be brief. If it is possible to cut a word out, always cut it out.

5   Never use the passive voice in your writing where you can use the active. (*Passive voice:* 'The disgraced CEO was told by the chairman of the board to exit through the back door.' *Active voice:* 'The chairman of the board told the disgraced CEO to exit through the back door.')

6   Don't use a foreign phrase, scientific or technical language, or industry jargon if you can think of an everyday equivalent, but do enlist the use of persuasive adjectives and metaphors.

7   These articles contain only your opinions, suggestions and viewpoints. Therefore, you do not need to undertake or include complicated or intricate research. However, including relevant examples and extremely brief case studies will add authority to your ideas and opinions.

8   Never make a sales pitch in an article for publication, as the editor will more likely than not reject it. Remember that magazines and journals make their money from selling advertising. Writing a veiled sales pitch under the guise of an editorial article won't pass muster.

9   Always include your contact email, website URL and blog URL.

CHAPTER 4

You're in the relationship business

There will always, one can assume, be need for some selling. But the aim of marketing is to make selling superfluous. The aim of marketing is to know and understand the customer so well that the product or service fits him/her and sells itself. Ideally, marketing should result in a customer who is ready to buy. All that should be needed then is to make the product or service available.
Peter Drucker

Marketing the old-fashioned way is irrelevant today. It's everyone's responsibility to market and promote the practice, especially the partners. Being the owner or a senior partner does not abrogate that person's responsibility to engage in marketing. Professional services is a relationship business—it's a marketing business. Nothing happens until somebody sells something. It may be the sale of a solution to a particular need, or the delivery of exceptional customer service. You do not need to cold call or walk the streets canvassing for business. But you do need to do something. Business acquisition doesn't just happen—you must make it happen.

In this chapter you learn how to:

- establish a unique brand
- employ public speaking to promote your practice
- utilise trade and professional associations
- handle the media.

The professional services industry is a hotchpotch of personalities and, interestingly, the stereotypes are changing. A couple of decades ago you could have defined lawyers and accountants as being drivers completely bereft of any marketing bent; recruiters, insurance agents and financial planners as expressive sales-type go-getters; human resources professionals consultants and bankers as amiables; and engineers and audiences as introverted analytics. Not so today. The younger generation of lawyers and accountants are acutely aware of the need to market and network. The issue for most professionals, however, remains that at no time during their undergraduate studies were they formally exposed to business development concepts of any type.

Derailed by mindsets

When accounting and legal firms speak with me about marketing, it's not unusual for the senior partners and directors to tell me they have already tried some or all of the things being suggested. No doubt in your profession you will have heard similar responses to advice you offer. Of course, you know for a fact that it would work if they applied themselves to implementing your strategies exactly as you have explained them. You have used the approach successfully with many clients previously, and you use the techniques yourself. You are fairly certain that 99 times out of 100 your recommendations will succeed. If only they would give it a go! The mindset of paradigms held as sacrosanct are usually rock-solid. You recognise them by the following characteristics:

- It is a very strongly held belief/conviction.

- It will feel absolutely true to the person with this mindset.

- They identify and are psychologically attached to the mindset.

- Disagreement with the mindset will often lead to
  negative outbursts.

- The mindset correlates with both actions and avoidance.

As an example, when I suggest to some professionals that they raise their fees and I happen to strike a mindset that insists the market won't allow this, I always hear the following types of responses:

- 'The market won't accept that in the current economy.'

- 'Our fees are benchmarked against the competition; if we raise our fees, we will lose clients to the competition.'

- 'We've built our reputation on being affordable.'

- 'Clients will walk if we do that.'

- 'Forget that idea. What else can we do to increase profits?'

What also must be recognised about mindsets is that we can all see them in other people, but rarely do we see them in ourselves. We have opinions based on experience, of course, and we have strong ideas about how we should operate. But we're certainly not stuck in any mindsets ourselves. There are two kinds of mindsets: constrictive and expansive. An expansive mindset isn't defensive, but rather is curious and interested about the possibilities. How might we do it better, make it grow, build it bigger? Superb performance and results come from expansive mindsets. A constrictive mindset sees problems, obstacles, issues and difficulties. A constrictive mindset insists on being right and has little interest in exploring, learning or growing. It thinks more about being safe and comfortable.

My experience is that many people in professional services are afraid to stand out from the crowd and behave differently, behave better, behave smarter than everyone else in their marketplace. 'Business is tough, competition is fierce and clients are unbending on price. We tried that during the Whitlam years, Ric, and it didn't work.' Yes it will. It's working for me and my clients. But before you learn the techniques and skills to implement my profit-building strategies, you must let go of your long-held beliefs about marketing.

Being successful draws attention to you, and some of that attention may be negative because others are jealous of your success and try to tear you down so you're back at their level of misery and mediocrity. Consequently, many people in professional services attempt to market themselves in ways that they perceive to be conservative and peer–acceptable. Hence, I've created the Whirlpool Marketing theory, which provides a myriad marketing options for professionals who are ambitious and enthusiastic to succeed in business. Some people in the professional services arena try so hard to win a new piece of business that they fail to secure a relationship with a new client. Marketing professional services is not the same as selling cars, computers or refrigerators (customers deciding primarily on price); neither is it like takeaway coffee, newsagencies or fast food (customers mainly wanting quick service).

You Can't Make This Up

In a world of noise we need to stand out from the crowd rather than blend in with the mosaic. How? A family restaurant in Poulsbo, Washington has created marketing magic by providing a discount for the patrons' well-behaved children!

On Friday, 1 February 2013, Laura King and her husband took their three children, aged two, three and eight, to an Italian restaurant in Poulsbo to enjoy an early-evening meal. The Washington couple was left stunned after their server handed them the bill—and they saw they had been given a $4 discount for their 'Well Behaved Kids'.

Any business, including a professional practice, could replicate this approach and create an appropriate gesture of goodwill. This is pure marketing genius. Great publicity, superb customer-relationship building, and positive word-of-mouth marketing are unquantifiable in their short- and long-term value to your organisation's success.

Establish a unique brand

What are the components that help support the brand of your professional practice? What can you do to establish a unique brand that honours the attributes you want to be identified with your firm? Each time a client or prospective customer comes into contact with some facet of your business it reflects on your practice and influences your brand. These facets include:

- stationery and letterhead
- website, email, blog and social media

- faxes, telephone, on-hold messages, voicemail and receptionists

- press releases, invoices and newsletters

- advertising, company vehicles, and employee grooming, dress and deportment

- sponsorships, charity involvement, trade shows and community events.

Radio interviews

Being interviewed on radio won't make you famous or generate hundreds of inquiries for your services. However, it will provide you with an opportunity to be recorded while being interviewed by a media professional, and the recording will be of the highest quality. You can then include this recording in your marketing collateral. It's very impressive to have a CD of a radio interview in your media/promotions/publicity kit.

There are many talk shows on radio (and television) but a relatively small amount of quality content. So you have a reasonably good chance of making an impression when you do get your chance. Marketing to producers and on-air talent is tough. They are busy people who don't return telephone calls or emails unless you're someone like Richard Branson. That said, if you have the patience and the diligence to make this a regular component of your Marketing Whirlpool, you will eventually be rewarded, either by persistence or by serendipity.

Today email is preferred over fax or traditional mail, although the higher-level radio shows should always receive your hard-copy media/promotional kit, including testimonials, booklet, CD and so on, to boost your credibility. Appreciate that journalists and media people don't have the time or probably the inclination to visit your website or download files. So provide them with everything they need and make it easy for them. Personalise your letters (don't automate them) and use the names of the on-air host or producer. Do not use: 'Attention: ABC Radio Business Show Producer'. If you can't put in the effort to research the producer's name, why would they expect you to make an effort to be current and cutting-edge in your research, knowledge and information?

Whirlpool Wisdom

- Articulate what listeners learn and how they will benefit.

- Be timely. Noticing current issues in the news and providing your alternate opinion in a challenging manner will get you noticed. Piggybacking on the headlines will always help.

- Never pay to be on a radio show. There's no point. You're rarely going to make money from it and any reputable radio station will not charge you. Don't be duped by the advent of internet radio programs, because in my opinion there's no one of merit listening to them.

Many radio interviews are transacted by telephone. This is a major bonus because there is no travel, you can be relaxing in your office or home study, you have your pad and pencil jotting notes to yourself to help you during the interview, and you can have a glass of water for when you inevitably get 'dry-mouth'. Do good work and the word may well spread, quickly. It took 18 months for me to be interviewed the first time on ABC Radio (Australia). After that, ABC knew I was 'safe' (regarding their rules of not mentioning brand names or being self-promotional), and now ABC journalists from around Australia regularly telephone me.

Employ public speaking to promote your practice

Speaking in public to business groups is a fine activity that achieves several objectives:

- It enhances your credibility by dint of the fact that you were invited to speak to the group.

- It provides additional exposure for you and your business at little or no cost.

- Speaking publicly creates a centricity around you as an expert and guarantees you attention-attraction during the networking session afterwards. People will gravitate to you.

- It positions you in front of prospective clients.

- During your presentation the audience is focused on only one person—you.

None of us has unlimited time, so we must be judicious with our decisions of where to speak, when to speak and what to speak about. Whether you're a professional speaker, delivering a presentation to stakeholders, or addressing a business group or association, knowing exactly what has to be delivered is vital to your success. By seeking answers to some straightforward questions, you will better understand what's required to guarantee the transfer of information that will most benefit the audience. Be certain that the content of your presentation focuses on the benefits of the professional service you offer, rather than the features. You want the audience to appreciate how your advice directly relates to the benefits they would receive.

Type of presentation: _____ (keynote/plenary/training session/sales presentation/breakfast, lunch or dinner talk*/client update/other)

Date: _____ Time: _____ # Attending: _____

1 What is the outcome sought for this presentation?

2 What do we want the audience to have achieved after the presentation?

3 How would you describe the target group we are talking about?

---

*Each has nuances that will affect your presentation style. People tend not to linger after a breakfast presentation as they need to get to their place of business. Therefore it's imperative that you prepare marketing collateral that is situated at every place setting, or at least at every table, for the attendees to be able to take away with them. A lunch presentation may or may not afford you networking opportunities directly after your presentation. A dinner talk is one of the most difficult from which to achieve acquisition opportunities. Generally the venues are loud and polluted with the clanging of crockery and cutlery. Attendees are more likely to consume alcohol, arrive late, leave early and talk while you're speaking.

4   What is the organisation's current challenge or this group's challenge?

5   How was it received? How effective was it?

6   What have been some of their major achievements in the past 12 months?

7   What have been some of their setbacks?

8   How would you describe the audience (skills, abilities, individual needs, experience)?

9   What are the areas of potential the audience need be able to tap into?

Marketing collateral you provide for attendees of any speaking presentation should follow a few simple rules:

1   Contact details should be printed on every page. Many times people attending will collect your brochure, handouts, booklets and photocopy them to disseminate to colleagues within their organisation. If your contact details are only on the last page, there is no guarantee that page will be included.

2   Marketing collateral should provide an inducement for people to contact you. This can be as simple as receiving a free report or perhaps a free consultation.

3   The marketing piece must directly relate to the content of your presentation.

4   The marketing piece should include a testimonial (if possible) from an instantly recognisable person who belongs to or identifies with the association or group to which you are presenting.

There's considerable value to be gained for your practice by speaking in front of your peers. Firstly, eliminate the mindset that they are your competition. Embrace the philosophy that there is an abundance of opportunity and more than enough business to be shared among you all. Secondly, depending upon your profession you may have skills and expertise that are non-competitive and complementary to the skills and expertise of your peers. This provides opportunity for those people who have now been exposed to you and your expertise to refer and recommend their clients to you for the areas of work their organisation does not provide. Thirdly, presenting to your fellow practitioners, who have congregated to listen to your thoughts and draw on your wisdom, brings cachet. Your clients would find it admirable that their professional adviser is the teacher, not the pupil.

Presenting and speaking in public should be a staple of the activity included in your Marketing Whirlpool. Given the opportunity to make a presentation once, exposing 50 people to your message, or conveying the same message 50 times to individual prospects, which would you choose? As a minimum, my recommendation to any professional practitioner is to make a public presentation at least once every two months. The more often you present, the better speaker you become. Table 4.1 shows a simple template for how to record your presentations during the year. This template has the information you require, and at a glance keeps you updated and current.

Table 4.1: template for recording presentations

Month	Group	Presentation	Contact	Done
Feb 2014	AICD	The Innovation Formula: Setting strategy people can actually use	Jane Whipp	✔
Mar 2014	CPA	Value-based Fees: Purposeful pricing that works for both you and your client	Marilyn Gunn	✔
Apr 2014	Qld Law Society	Whirlpool Marketing: Grow your practice in just 30 minutes a day	Giles Watson	
May 2014	College of Law	The Hidden Factor: How to see what the competition cannot	A-M David	
June 2014	PwC BNE	Change 601: Pragmatic solutions for organisational change	Rob Ashley	

Sponsorship opportunities

Having the naming rights to certain events can be a magical publicity tool. Sponsorship can favour the brave but other times leave you lost and deflated, wondering why you received nothing from your investment. Buying sponsorship is fraught with danger if you are not diligent in assessing the entire package. Sponsorship of most events rarely comes cheaply, so if you do decide to contribute funds, it's worth assigning responsibility to micromanage your contribution and promised benefits to an individual staff member. Sponsorship sales agents are all very fine people I'm sure, but frequently I hear my clients complaining that promises made were never kept although the cash certainly was. Once you've made an assessment that you believe the sponsorship will provide you with the appropriate level of exposure and contact with prospective clients, you must treat this like any other marketing initiative.

- Know your costs.

- Know what you expect to receive in return for your investment.

- Get it in writing, duly signed.

- Assign resources to the sponsorship as you would any other business project.

- Strategise how you will maximise the results of your involvement.

- Plan your promotions and publicity to capitalise on your involvement and investment—before, during and after the event.

- Plan how your practice will be able to follow up on all opportunities within five days of the event.

- Plan what your practice will do to follow up again within 30 days of the event.

- Take responsibility for maximising your involvement by gaining media coverage for your organisation's sponsorship.

Do not assume that the event coordinators, the host association or the sponsorship sales people will proactively do any of this for you. The likelihood is that if you don't do it, nobody else will and your sponsorship dollars will have been wasted.

As an aside, I am frequently asked about how to decline a request to sponsor an event (or a donation request). Many professionals feel embarrassed by the pressure placed on them by association executives or sponsorship salespeople. In fairness to you, it's impossible to grant every request for sponsorship by the associations and business groups to which you belong. My advice is for you to be firm but polite. Usually the people reaching out to you are just doing their job, or they may be volunteers giving their time to assist the organisation they are representing. Keep your response brief and don't engage further once you've politely declined. Explain that you never grant oral requests for sponsorships and that any request must be made in writing. Here is a template you can adopt or adapt:

> Thank you for inviting us to sponsor your race day on the Gold Coast next month.
>
> I think sponsoring corporate events and functions is an excellent idea and can provide much enjoyment for everyone involved on the day, with the possibility of new connections that may lead to business discussions.
>
> Unfortunately, our sponsorship budget for this year has been allocated for quite some time. Each year we allocate significant money, which is claimed almost immediately!
>
> All the best with your race day plans. I look forward to reading about the success of your event in the local media.

Trade and professional associations

Your involvement in trade and professional associations has the potential to provide you with exposure that might otherwise be cost prohibitive. Do not limit yourself to your industry. In fact, I'm recommending something quite different. That is that you infiltrate the trade and professional associations of which your clients are members. Most if not all of these groups will allow for associate membership where you don't have to be an active professional in the industry. This allows you to regularly network with your ideal audience. But networking is only dabbling at the surface of the Marketing Whirlpool. There are many other ways to involve yourself and your practice in an association:

- Write for the publications owned by the association.
- Take an advertisement in the association directory.
- Take an advertisement in the association magazine.

- Volunteer for the committee and ensure it is a highly visible role. Event programming, accreditation and continuing education, and membership are just a few examples.

- Become an office bearer.

- Sponsor key events.

- Purchase a booth or exhibit in the trade show area at the national conference.

- Offer to mentor members.

Whirlpool action: Make a concerted effort to become active and positively contribute to the association and its members.

Articles written for trade and professional associations must get noticed if they are to be worth your time investment. Therefore, write strong and passionate contributions that stand out from the crowd by being contrary to conventional wisdom. So long as you can justify your stance, arguing with the flavour of the day will draw people to you. The benefit of article writing is that you're not corralled into a narrow market, and you can extend your existing business reach into new markets easily (see figure 4.1).

Figure 4.1: article writing for associations

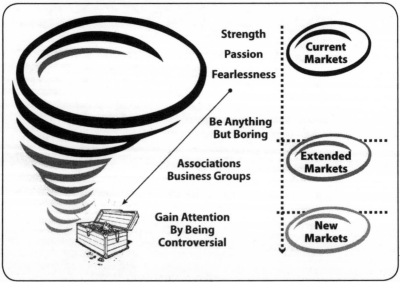

Best Practices

The objective of Whirlpool Marketing is to develop deep and trusting relationships with buyers who can authorise payment for your professional services. Senior executives and bright minds have little respect for sycophants or 'hesitants', but do respect being challenged by insightful and intelligent thinkers. If you believe the client is wrong, or could consider a better alternative, have the courage to speak up. Counterintuitively, you'll gain more acceptance by the people who can pay for your expertise.

How to elicit emotional priorities

I was asked why I so frequently post photographs and stories of other people—clients, colleagues, delegates and so on—on my business blog. 'It's your business blog. Shouldn't you be promoting you and what you do rather than stories and photos of colleagues and clients?' When someone says they took photos of the business conference, what do you immediately look for? That's right. Photographs of yourself. When someone says they took photos of the end-of-year party, what do you look for? Photos with you in them. It's smart business to feature the photos, stories and examples of your clients and customers. Are you telling the stories of your customers? Everyone loves to look at something and say, 'That's me!'

How to handle the media

The best advertising your business can receive is positive press coverage. It costs you nothing and offers an objective, third-party assessment of your business, which people are more likely to trust than a paid advertisement. The media can be a valuable ally. Developing relationships with local, national and international media can be a great way of improving your profile. How can you form effective relationships for the media?

1   **Never ever say no.** Most media organisations are running on tight schedules and their stress levels are high. If you can't personally help them, try putting them in touch with

someone who can. The more positive your interactions with them are, the more likely they are to come back to you.

2 **Be accommodating.** Put yourself out to help the media. Maintaining a successful relationship with a media organisation requires mutual respect.

3 **Be available.** If you've made contact with the media through a press release, make certain you're available to comment when you say you will be.

4 **Be proactive.** Most media outlets are always on the lookout for new content or stories. Take advantage of this — call them, email them, drop in and visit. If the media don't know who you are, you won't get coverage. Know when to stop though — don't call them every day, and don't try to pass soft news stories off as hard news. Be honest.

5 **Take opportunities when they're offered.** If someone offers you a chance to be involved in a meeting where media journalists can familiarise themselves with you, or offers a review or interview, take it. A good review is priceless. Word-of-mouth works within media circles too — if you give one journalist a good experience, they'll pass it on to other people in their circles.

6 **If at first you don't succeed, keep trying.** You're never guaranteed media coverage (unless you're paying for it). There's always the chance that something bigger or better than your story will come up at the last minute. Don't take missed opportunities personally.

7 **Target niche publications.** Exposure in the national media is fantastic, but it won't always convert into immediate business. Targeting niche magazines and programs that deal uniquely with the industry is a great way to ensure the people who read the article will take notice. People who read niche publications have chosen to read them with a particular interest and purpose in mind.

8 **Never ever say anything in front of the media you don't want quoted.** There is no such thing as 'off the record' — if a piece of information is appealing enough the

media will bite. It doesn't matter how good your relationship is with them—every journalist wants a scoop.

9 **Always thank the media for positive coverage they give you.** Journalists are just like everyone else—they appreciate positive feedback. If they feel warm and fuzzy towards you it certainly won't do your relationship any harm.

From the Front Lines

In August 2013 I was the opening and closing keynote speaker for the CPA Fiji Congress in Nadi. I was quoted by the two leading Fiji newspapers seven times in five days. How?

1   I introduced myself to the media and made myself freely available to them at any time during the three days I was at the congress.

2   One of the reporters asked if she could impose upon my time and sit with me during breakfast. Of course, I agreed.

3   When I was on a panel of five people for the press conference, I remained calm, didn't interrupt and waited for the media to ask me specific questions. Then I hit them with provocative, contrarian, intelligent perspectives that were anything but ordinary or expected. They soaked it up.

After the formal press conference, two journalists from competing newspapers asked me for further comment. As we concluded, one of the journalists said, 'Mr Willmot, you make it so effortless and easy for us to speak with you and ask questions. Thank you for being so kind.' The Fijians are beautiful people and see the good in everyone, but the point remains valid: Make it easy and effortless for people to speak with you and they will love you for it and want more. No other speaker on the program, and there were many, was quoted in the Fijian press other than the CPA officials. Doesn't that tell you something?

CHAPTER 5

Establish great acquisition sources and dominate your market

Marketing is getting someone who has a need to know,
like and trust you.
Jon Jantsch (author of *Duct Tape Marketing*)

We burst into our profession with gusto. Our enthusiasm is contagious. Referrals come our way and we continue along the path of least resistance without thinking too deeply about what our strategy should be. Soon, however, business acquisition plateaus and we're lost as to where to find new sources of business. University didn't prepare us for selling our services and we're unsure how to go about attracting and acquiring clients.

In this chapter you learn how to:

- identify acquisition channels

- learn who has the authority to engage you

- provide value early

- develop a memorable brand that will attract clients to you

- reach out laterally to maximise your efforts

- retain the client and their business.

It's easy to get excited when we first start our professional practice. Many of the people we went to university with give us their business and refer others along the way. But after the initial burst, business plateaus—or worse, it withers. It's not that we intended to rely on our friends and acquaintances as the sole source of our business, but it quickly became the path of least resistance, especially given we were not taught how to market for business while completing our technical degree. Most of us tend to hit the wall around the three-year mark, because by then we have exhausted the referrals and introductions we can extract from our sphere of influence. It's at this point that many look to acquiring a partner, merging with another practice or finding a salaried position.

Some professionals will complain that they're a lawyer (or accountant or financial planner), not a salesman. Of course you didn't become a lawyer to spend your days marketing and selling. The first point to make is that marketing and selling are not the same. Secondly, no matter how technically brilliant you are in your profession, nothing happens until you win a client. If you expect to continue winning new clients beyond your initial two or three years, you will need to market yourself. It's as simple as that. If you have sensational value to offer, then you are not 'selling', because you would be remiss not to assertively provide this value. The world of professional advisers has evolved and it's the rare professional who does not need to engage in business development. You may be in a firm that cannot rely solely on a few business development managers (or rainmakers) to acquire new work and provide projects for everyone else. Or perhaps you're a solo-preneur and if you don't attract and acquire new business, nobody else will. Either way, you must become involved in growing the firm, but the thought of having to market and sell makes you anxious, distressed and uneasy. You love what you do, but you don't like being a salesman.

You're not alone. In fact, you've got plenty of company. I hear it repeatedly in conversations I have with clients, seminar delegates and conference participants:

- I didn't become an accountant (or lawyer or financial planner…) to wind up in sales.

- Selling gets in the way of developing trusting relationships.

- I just want to do great work for my clients and allow word-of-mouth to do the rest.

- I never had to do marketing and selling in the past.

- My clients won't respect me if I try to sell more to them.

- I don't have time to market with everything else that's on my plate.

- Selling is anathema to being a professional.

- I wasn't trained to do business development. I don't know what's needed, and I don't want to look cheap.

- It's not in me to be a salesperson.

Here's a tip: The skills that make you a great technical expert are the same ones you need to dramatically increase your business results—all that's required is for you to sharpen those skills and implement them effectively. When you work with your clients you:

- ask questions

- provide expert opinions

- work hard

- make yourself accessible

- build creative solutions

- deliver on what you promise

- develop relationships

- keep your clients' best interest in mind

- introduce clients to new ideas, helping them to see a better way.

That's exactly what's required to become successful in attracting and acquiring new business. It's not about manipulating anyone to buy something they don't need. It's about helping clients and prospects find solutions to their needs and providing value with care and consideration.

Whirlpool Marketing is effective for both active and passive marketing strategies. Successful professional practices engage in both types and ensure the marketing is focused, driven and continually evolving. Successful marketing is not a set-and-forget scenario. By intelligently implementing your Marketing Whirlpool you will achieve a leading market position and make it difficult for the competition to move in on your niche. It requires effort, forethought and discipline. Carefully planning the strategy and implementing the action steps, you will dominate your territory while expanding your own market reach.

From the Front Lines

'No one likes being rejected. Every time I was discussing potential business with the client, I was in fear of being rejected. The epiphany came when I considered that my clients would feel the same way. I pretended to be more confident, as if I were assessing whether I wanted the client or not. I felt better, I behaved better, and my clients became more flexible and respectful of my advice and me.'

—Sion Ford, Director, Lab Distributors

Acquisition channels

When was the last time you said to yourself, 'I want fewer clients'? Defining strategies and activities to uncover new sources of clients is an ever-shifting process. Some sources of business have been around forever; others are situational and in time will disappear, never to be seen again. The acquisition channels I use today in my practice (see figure 5.1) are very different from those I employed to start from a zero base in 2004. No matter what your profession or ideal client, or the demographics, there are sources that will continue to give you faithful service. The four acquisition channels I describe next exemplify how purposeful planning and laser-like focus can produce superior returns to generalised (and sometimes lazy) approaches. If these acquisition sources are already firmly rooted in your practice, delivering the results you require, you're welcome to skip ahead, no questions asked.

Figure 5.1: acquisition channels

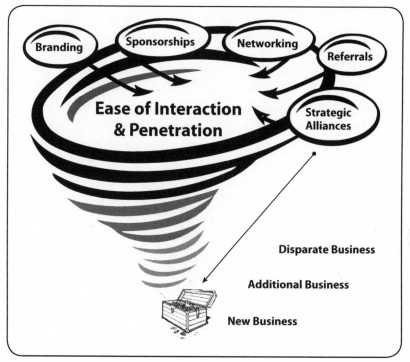

1 Endorsement marketing

Early in my accounting career I was introduced to an organisational psychologist named Tim Dalmau, who leased office space on a mezzanine floor of the chartered accounting firm where I worked. In later life I would come to work for Tim in his consultancy group for more than six years. Tim is an amazingly successful consultant with tremendous expertise and superb selling skills, a truly global consultant who has consulted to some of the most prestigious companies for more than three decades. When people ask him how he manages to attract the attention of global CEOs in organisations like Caltex, Ernst & Young and BHP, he explains that he can track almost 90 per cent of his business back to a dozen or so people he met decades earlier. These people have risen through the ranks of their organisations, have transferred to divisions around the world or have moved into entirely new organisations. His relationship with these people has enabled them to continually endorse and promote his consulting work.

Being endorsed is one of the strongest ways you can be promoted to people and organisations who have yet to learn of the value you deliver. With the leverage of working with independent organisations and people who readily commend and attest to your skills and competencies, you can move the world. Continually scan the horizon and your business landscape for complementary organisations whose endorsement of you to their clients and markets will bolster your repute before you've even arrived.

Whirlpool action: List the most highly regarded organisations and associations that are non-competitive and complementary to your practice. Outline three key areas that are central to your fundamental value proposition and have unique significance to the clients and members of those organisations and associations. Investigate who is on the executive leadership teams, search your contacts and find out who among them may be able to introduce you to those people. Through introduction or direct approach, reach out to the executive leadership in those organisations and associations, and present a clear business case for how your practice can work with them to provide additional value to their clients and members to which they would otherwise not be exposed.

2 Professional and trade associations

Many advise reaching out to professional and trade associations, and with just cause. Achieving the desired results requires an understanding of the nuances of a genuine connection with the members. It makes little sense to increase your workload through involvement in the associations where your clients are members, and not receive a return on investment (time being your most significant asset). I am increasingly approached by legal firms with requests that I present to them and consult on matters such as pricing strategies and business development. Financial planning organisations ask for my help in business structuring, branding and making the transition from commission to fee-for-service. Accounting practices are growing beyond compliance work and are now offering advice on estate planning and self-managed superannuation funds, business consulting and much more. Accountants throughout Australia, New Zealand and Asia are seeking my advice to help them implement these new business services and to properly transition away from hourly billing.

These three industry associations are in the midst of significant change and transition. Their members are my ideal clients. Therefore, the more I can place my intellectual property in front of them by speaking and publishing, the more likely I will receive enquiries about what I do and how I can help them. The strategy for you is clear: identify your ideal clients, learn what changes are affecting their business, address the areas where you have the expertise to provide the best solutions for them to cope with those changes, and formalise your intellectual property for consumption by the executives of those professional and trade associations to which those ideal clients belong. What you present to the professional trade associations of your ideal clients needs to be acutely connected to you and your practice, so you are seen as *the* resource for the solutions they seek.

Whirlpool action: List your best, most favoured six clients. Ascertain the characteristics and traits of each client, and the services you provide to them, and determine what they have in common. Investigate and list the professional and trade associations and the business groups to which they belong. Discover and list the magazines, journals and trade organs they subscribe to and read. List the business events and conferences they attend. You now have a boilerplate of where you want to speak, network and publish to position yourself as a person of interest to those ideal clients who need what you have. This is a pragmatic and targeted approach, which is what's required for your involvement to be successful.

3 Universities, business schools and higher education

When I opened the doors of my OD consultancy in 2004, I was starting with a zero base. For the first six months I was not rushed off my feet with work. I chose to volunteer my services as a guest lecturer at colleges, universities and business schools for one-off lessons on such topics as leadership, change management, strategy, and organisational psychology and behaviour. It was a way for me to keep busy, maintain a sense of contribution and create new intellectual property. Nine years later, some of those undergraduate and postgraduate students are approaching me to consult in the organisations where they now work. People in professional practice—like you and me—bring to these educational classes pragmatic, real-world experiences that academics are not exposed to. Theory is important; experiential learning is a requisite.

Whirlpool action: List all the educational facilities within your area that teach classes for which your subject matter has relevance and application. Develop a brief of collateral and post this to the heads of department, with an attached letter volunteering your services to deliver one-off lectures around your expertise.

4 Online learning

People in remote locations are significantly disadvantaged in their quest for knowledge improvement. For many of these people technology has been a saviour. So long as they have a computer with access to the internet, and the self-discipline to undertake self-paced learning, they have the opportunity to acquire the knowledge, information, diagnostics and tools they need to implement into their business. This is a real and growing market, bringing about dramatic change in education and the foundation for a new pillar of your professional practice. Xero cloud accounting and bookkeeping software has exploded onto the landscape and is set to dramatically change the financial operations of many businesses and industry sectors. I foresee a time in the not-too-distant future when it will become a requirement for commercial organisations to upload their business accounts through cloud software on a monthly basis, and they will pay their taxation obligations within 15 days after the close of every month. The business of accountants is soon to change. Webinars and teleconferences have become commonplace; online degrees are offered by all the major universities; professional associations are recording training workshops and uploading them to the internet for members to download and view at their leisure. My own mentor program provides unlimited access to me via telephone, fax, email, online forums and live webinars. These webinars are also recorded and made available in the members-only area of my website.

Whirlpool action: What components of your professional practice, knowledge and expertise can be converted for suitable use on technology platforms? What new intellectual property could be created or adapted from what you already own for suitable use on technology platforms? List three disparate knowledge bases from your practice, brainstorm how they could effectively be adopted for online learning, outsource the process of conversion to a technological platform, and then aggressively market.

Embracing a more detailed examination of how you implement acquisition strategies in practice will save you time, money and anguish. If you consider the marketing worth doing, then it's worth doing right. Take a purposely sophisticated approach to understand how best to make any marketing activity singularly successful. The additional time you invest upfront in the preparation and planning to make the marketing activity pertinent and on target will save substantially more time in the end. The effectiveness of any and all marketing is in the preparation.

Other examples of lead generation activities that assist in the acquisition of new business are:

- networking
- public relations
- sponsorship
- advertising
- direct mail
- alliances
- community and charity involvement
- partnering with professional colleagues
- promoting to your suppliers
- subcontracting
- becoming the middle man for other subcontractors
- referrals
- seminars and workshops
- website
- passive listings

- speaking at chambers of commerce
- creating products from your IP for sale
- taking a leadership role in a trade association
- attending trade shows
- accepting interns.

Best Practices

Your marketing is at its best when you determine what your marketplace needs. Develop an information campaign that describes why you're the best solution, and position that information where those clients who need it will find it. The selling activity required of you then is simply to offer options on how the client can engage you, and to let them choose for themselves how they'd like to proceed. Your Whirlpool Marketing projects should be designed in a three-tiered process.

1 Objective
   a. Decide on the project.
   b. Decide on the targets of opportunity.
   c. Choose alliances and/or promotional channels to power your whirlpool to gain exposure.

2 Market
   a. Divide your targets of opportunity into three distinct areas.
   b. Prioritise each of those three areas in terms of loyalty to and connection with your practice.
   c. Design a three-step process to move prospective clients deeper into your whirlpool.

3 Methodology
   a. Design and implement strong positioning media and brand recognition collateral.
   b. Ascertain at what depths of the whirlpool the positioning and branding will be placed. Implement Whirlpool Marketing activities, actions and tasks that will create opportunities and attract new business. Assign responsibility for the activities, with deadlines for individuals within your practice (as any burden shared becomes easier to carry).

Projects should be established to support the three stages of ongoing business development growth for your firm: 50 per cent focused on short-term results, 30 per cent on mid-term, and 20 per cent on long-term (see table 5.1). Consider these figures to be arbitrary and for illustration purposes only. Your professional practice will have its own nuances with regard to the type of expertise you deliver, the types of clients who are ideal for your business, and so on.

Table 5.1: the three stages of business development growth

Short-term	Mid-term	Long-term
50%	30%	20%
3 months	6–9 months	12+ months

Who has the authority to engage you?

The professional services business, as the name implies, is all about service. To provide excellent service you have to be in the company of your clients. Accountants, lawyers, financial advisers, human resource consultants and recruiters aren't hired until they've met personally with the client. This is a relationship-based business. Knowing this to be true, why then do we allow ourselves to be scuttled by non-buyers within the client organisation? If you're an industrial relations consultant it's easy to believe you may be hired by the human resources manager. Although these are fine people who make significant contributions to their organisation, most do not have the authority or the budget to authorise your engagement or payment. Human resources managers have the ability to reject you and refuse your advances, but they rarely have the permission to sign your contract and deposit the fees into your bank account.

However, you may not always need to secure approval from the business owner or the CEO. Executive and senior management will sometimes have ultimate authority to engage your services. Asking the question, 'Are you the decision maker?' is a little forward, and assuredly ineffective. I suggest an approach such as, 'Who else would you like to consult before making a decision?'

Or, 'Do we need to meet with anyone else to get authorisation for payment of my fees?' And finally, 'If we agree on everything today, can we shake hands and start on the project tomorrow?' The responses, and the speed of response, will tell you if this person is the decision maker. I appreciate you may perceive this as being a little too assertive, and perhaps even tough, but if you are dealing with the right person they'll immediately tell you. If you're not, their hesitancy alone will make plain that someone else has the cheque-signing authority.

Why you must provide value early

It's imperative that you provide value early when developing relationships with potential clients. From their perspective, they are overworked, and changing priorities increase the pressure and anxiety they feel every day. Your clients crave simplicity in their work. By providing them with value early in the relationship to help them understand why you're the best person to be helping, you simplify their decision making, which raises their opinion of you. When I speak of this, people are aghast that I'm recommending they give away their ideas for free. Their concern is that if they give away their advice, then there is no need for the client to pay for it.

I'm not proposing that you provide comprehensive in-depth advice, solutions or recommendations, but rather that you share your insights and observations that are relevant and current to the real issues facing your clients right at this moment. My caveat is that with the prevalent use of the internet and social media, there is now an amorphous mess of articles and opinions that provide little value but drown out good information. Therefore, purposely present only the highest quality intellectual property in specific media that positions you in front of your ideal clients. Reinforce the adage 'quality over quantity'. There's no point in your throwing more berley on the waters. The purpose of providing these overviews is to allow your audience to appreciate that there are ways for them to improve their lot that they haven't yet considered, and that you are the right person to advise them on which to choose and how to implement these alternatives. You may see this advice as counterintuitive to the financial practicalities of business. Not so. The psychology of this approach is that when prospective buyers have been exposed to your smarts and they can recognise that you have unique and worthwhile intellectual firepower that will substantively benefit their business, they will assign even greater value to you and your advice. This translates into higher fee levels and a smoother passage to your engagement agreement.

Prospective clients who have been exposed to your intellectual heft will more quickly and readily accept your acumen and professional services. Any conversation you have with these people is now focused on how you can help them and the value they will receive from your interventions, with no further concern as to whether you are the right person to engage. They've already decided that you're the person to help; your part is now to provide them with the best options to make it happen. You have negated the need for any agonising 'sales talk', and moved directly to discussions of your professional guidance.

This process fast-tracks the journey of suspect to prospect to client, and eliminates the anxiety of wondering if you'll get the business. Languishing as a prisoner of hope is not a pleasant process. Appreciate that this highway of acquisition eliminates comparisons between you and any competitors because the prospective client has sought you out in preference to your competitors and has already determined that you have the answers to their problems. When you continually position appropriate intellectual property, you build momentum for the ongoing attraction of you and your work. To refuse or ignore this key strategy is negligent and costly.

Develop a memorable brand that will attract clients to you

The brand of your professional practice and your personal brand contribute to the emotional reaction and attachment your clients experience when they interact with you. Professional services are highly competitive nowadays, even in the legal profession. Television advertising by legal firms perfectly makes this point. It is, therefore, more critical than ever that firms differentiate themselves from their competition. Future success depends on standing out from the crowd rather than blending in with the mosaic. Your branding, if done well, will capture the attention of your marketplace and potential buyers. Many professionals in smaller firms shudder at the thought of expensive advertising campaigns and cannot justify in their own mind the costs involved. But creating a brand can be done without the outlay of hundreds of thousands of dollars in advertising.

Your brand is what you represent, what you stand for, the values and principles you hold sacrosanct. It's not posturing, pretending or posing. It's about the real you, who you are on rainy days and Sundays, consistently, and what you project as being the benchmark of your personal attributes and performance. Within the corporate brand of your practice you will also have your individual brand, which directly reflects you as a person. Managing your personal/individual brand (and who you're working to become) is of vital importance. In the social media world it can be decimated in 140 characters or less. And just in case you are under the misconception that you don't have a brand, you do. It's just that it's not you who is driving, but rather your competitors.

Branding is formed and informed by your dress code, your business card, your correspondence, your work ethic, your choice of language, your tone of voice, even your body language. These are all touch-points with product, service and relationship, and they influence the impressions made by the marketplace. Regardless of whether you are a veteran or neophyte, you must focus and work on your brand and the brand of your practice to ensure they exemplify the image, status and cachet you desire and expect. Prove to yourself and your marketplace by your behaviours that you're the best choice. To learn how you may create a distinguishable brand, consider the reasons why you yourself have:

- trusted someone rapidly—even on first meeting

- immediately purchased a service you had not consciously known you needed

- changed your mind about a firmly held belief

- taken a call or responded to a letter from someone previously unknown to you

- responded enthusiastically to a new idea

- allowed someone to take an hour of your time.

All of these things and more occur because you've been suitably impressed by the person or the circumstances that brought about the opportunity to engage. As you work to create your brand identity, think from the outside in and focus on what would impress you; what would it take for this to influence your behaviour and engage you?

If you're wondering what is currently contributing to your brand, you will find the answers in the attributes and specific points you most frequently emphasise in your marketing collateral and interpersonal contact. The results you've achieved for existing and previous clients, as told by them, is another great source of brand identification. The latter provides you with your best information because it is what the buyers of your services are saying about you rather than what you are saying about yourself. Using the language of your most satisfied clients to develop your brand will resonate most with potential new clients. That language contains the elements of what attracts clients to you and is the most powerful language in all of your marketing. As you analyse your client testimonials, and the informal comments of your clients about you, look for those points that relate to the four Ps:

1 Promise of real business outcomes and results.

2 Personality of you, your people and your practice.

3 Position in the marketplace regarding your expertise, brilliance and service.

4 Perception of how you improve the condition of the client, such as increased performance, decreased pain, elimination of stress and new growth.

Whether you like it or not, the creation, growth and maintenance of your brand is a key component to your success over the long term. You are constantly being judged by the marketplace. What's your appearance like? Are you well dressed and suitably groomed? Do you look successful? People have said, 'How I wear my hair or how I dress has no bearing on my professional competency. Clients judge me only on the work I do'. Perhaps that's true, but consider the message you are sending about yourself into the marketplace and how people who do not yet know you perceive that. Nobody is going to trust a dentist with bad teeth. Prospective clients won't feel comfortable with a shabbily dressed lawyer. It will be difficult to believe the admonitions of an overweight dietician.

To develop, grow and maintain your brand—and ascertain where your greatest strengths lie—answer these questions to generate a checklist of brand elements:

- **What do you do?** You can make all the promises you like, but if you don't deliver, your promises are worthless. For example, claiming a customer service standard of guaranteed punctuality and then being late for appointments is an immediate contradiction that hurts your brand. As Ralph Waldo Emerson said, 'Your actions speak so loudly, I cannot hear what it is you say'. Be mindful that this speaks to your attitudes beyond punctuality. It reflects on whether you can be trusted in anything you say. Can you be depended on, no matter what? Is your word your bond?

- **What are your client surveys telling you?** Is there a pattern to the feedback and answers? Are there similarities in the language and comments that clients make to you through formal surveys and in face-to-face meetings? Is there a general trend in the results and outcomes achieved for your clients? If you are not already utilising client surveys, there's never been a better time to start than now.

- **What are the client testimonials telling you?** Do the formal and informal testimonials you receive contain a theme that speaks well to your expertise and competency? These are the people who have paid for your professional services, what specifically do they say about you and your work? And if you haven't been asking for testimonials, it's not too late. You can start today by personally contacting all of your clients of the past 6–12 months. Explain that you would greatly appreciate their making the time to drop you a brief note about the benefits and results they've received by employing your services.

- **What do the people who are referred to you say?** Have you noticed specific language that prospective new clients use when they contact you after being recommended by another person? Is there a particular reason that seems prevalent as to why you are referred and recommended? What is the common thread in unsolicited referrals and recommendations?

- **How do you communicate?** Your offices may be immaculate, your printing and stationery exquisite, and your marketing collateral of great quality, but you also need excellent communication skills to support all of these efforts. Do you have good posture? Do you emit enthusiasm and confidence? Are you comfortable making good eye contact and do you genuinely listen to people? Is your choice of language professional, articulate, pragmatic and clear? Remember that good communication is 25 per cent transmitting and 75 per cent receiving.

- **What IP produces the best results?** Analyse the dissemination of your intellectual property and quantify what is giving you the best bang for your buck. Have you measured more successful results from radio interviews given than from trade association articles published? Do you receive better results by being published in state-based magazines rather than national ones? Do you receive a higher number of enquiries when you provide information about cost reduction as opposed to revenue production? What are the topics where you have gained the most traction? What issues give you easier access to the media? Where and what do you receive the most interest from and about?

- **What are your website statistics telling you?** What pages of your website are most frequently visited? What content on your website is most widely read? Which case studies, position statements or articles are downloaded most? (Ignore the statistics relating to any push-marketing inducements that you've engaged in.)

- **What component of your whirlpool works best?** Is there a particular activity or a specific pillar of advice that attracts more prospects than others? In all of your marketing activity where is the greatest centrifugal force? Where is the swiftest speed of conversion from prospect to client?

- **Where is your technical edge?** What makes you more qualified than your competitors in a specific area of your service offerings? What makes you the best? This is not about braggadocio, but rather clearly iterating the skill and expertise that clients need and you do exceptionally well. If you're expecting people to buy you and your services and accept your advice, you must convince them that their confidence in you is justified. Give the marketplace the information they require to make an informed decision on choosing the best professional for their circumstances.

- **What do your peers say?** What do your colleagues and peers say about you and your expertise that differentiates you in their mind? Are you recognised for specific achievement or success? Are you identified with one particular client? Do your colleagues pigeonhole you in a specific area of expertise? How are you introduced by them to strangers?

- **What's your written correspondence like?** Writing is an art that explains much about who you are. Your written communication must be compelling, effective and pithy. The letters you write can be a governing factor for prospective clients. Although emails are less formal than hard-copy letters, you must still be vigilant in regard to spelling, punctuation and grammar. Any typos can cause you to be perceived as unprofessional and/or uneducated; or, worse still, your mistakes could be ascribed to laziness. Every piece of correspondence has the capacity to support the brand you want and an image that sells.

Based on your responses to this checklist you can ascertain where your branding is strongest. There will be a common thread through all this and it will relate directly to the results you've been able to achieve for your clients. Contained within your responses you will be able to identify the highest potential appeal for attracting new clients. As you move through the checklist it will become clearer where your brand identity is at its strongest and where potential clients will ascribe your value for them. You may not realise it yet, but by the end of the process you will come to appreciate the immense value you bring to the table.

When you take an introspective look at your brand, ask yourself if you're providing a return on investment that will convince the client to engage and pay for you and your expertise. Does your brand reflect the value you offer? Is the value significant enough to persuade prospective clients that they want to know more about you and how you can help them?

Whirlpool Wisdom

The sooner you start on creating your brand identity, the sooner you'll recoup a return on investment. Rome wasn't built in a day and neither is a brand. The tactics you should implement to develop your brand identity include, but are not limited to, the following behaviours:

- Be helpful—you have to give to get.

- Be sincere and build genuine, trusting relationships.

- Be memorable for all the right reasons—become an object of interest to others.

- Stay in touch with clients, prospects, peers and alliances.

- Cultivate with patience while keeping focused on your objective.

Reach out laterally to maximise your efforts

Ted Turner, the founder of CNN, said, 'Early to bed, early to rise, work like heck and publicise.' Richard Branson and Donald Trump both have a genius for maximising the reach of their brand to a point where their names are aligned with whatever they do. They have many diverse and disparate businesses, but their brand is so strong that all of their marketing attaches to them as individuals, making their name a brand with enormous power and reach. If your name has become a brand, protect it and magnify the effect through continuous promotion and whirlpool attraction.

To maximise the lateral reach of your marketing and promotion, you must perpetuate the visibility, recognition, quality and reputation of your professional practice and your people. Don't be afraid to draw attention to yourself. Fearless marketing that distinguishes you from the competition, when supported by client testimonials, intellectual property and measurable results, accelerates the power and attraction. Be everywhere that your clients are—publish in the journals and magazines they read, network and attend the events they do, speak before the associations and business groups to which they belong. It's impossible to deliver too much value. It's your sand pit—jump in and play.

There are many instances of organisations creating elite membership for customers who are willing to pay for special privilege. Airlines reward first-class passengers and significant frequent flyers with private lounges. Hotels provide executive club access to guests staying in the more expensive suites. Professional services firms can create similar advantages for their best clients, and appropriately charge an additional fee for the extra services and benefits.

Members of my private coaching and mentoring program cajoled me into providing a monthly newsletter that only current and past members would be eligible to receive. I was also regularly providing these alumni with research, diagnostics and business tools that I was not making freely available anywhere else. Responding to individual requests for these diagnostics and tools was time-consuming and inefficient. A repository, accessible only by username and password, was created on my website so the coaching and mentoring alumni could access the materials at their leisure. When I informed a coaching client about the repository and how she could gain access she quickly responded that she would have been willing to pay extra for it. Then it hit me: I can sell this service as a subset offering to clients who want access to the information but have not paid to be coached by me. Sometimes it pays to be lucky.

You will achieve greater lateral reach if your marketing is written for the prospects you want to attract, rather than yourself. What looks good to you is not necessarily effective for your desired audience. This mistake is made frequently by professional services firms. An idea is hatched, the principal or managing partner gets excited, a few staff give it the thumbs up and they run with the ball. When it fails to produce results, no one can understand why. In Australia, motor vehicle manufacturers Ford and Holden survived only through government funding in the billions of dollars. One of the reasons for their inability to attract sufficient customers was that they built the cars management liked but failed to build the types of cars Australians wanted to drive. Ensure your focus is on the markets you want to reach and test your strategies on that target market. Even if you are a sole trader, marketing research is necessary, and it isn't a one-off project. Market research needs to be incorporated into your marketing system and it needs to be ongoing.

To further extend your reach within your markets, the clients you are engaging need to be clear about how the additional services being offered will provide substantively greater benefits to their business. Any opaqueness, confusion or question marks in their mind, even for a second, and they have moved on. The opportunity is lost and rarely does it return. Don't be cute or clever with the messages you send to the marketplace about your additional service offerings. Make it simple and very clear. Cute and clever has a reference point now with spam. Don't let prospective or existing clients place you into that category.

There is no priority in the tactics you can apply to produce lateral reach, although you will definitely discover which tactics produce better results and are more important to your practice. Here are 12 targeted tactics to use to leverage your existing business and extend your business reach laterally:

1 **Do a sensational job.** This may seem to be a no-brainer, and naturally everyone believes the services they provide are the epitome of quality excellence. At some point,

circumstances will spin out of your control and the possibility of sub-par performance will infiltrate your work. And the decisions you make will affect your relationship, and future potential business, with that client forever.

2 **Differentiate yourself.** If you're just like everyone else, how can you expect to be chosen in preference to your competition, or to define your practice as a premium service delivery organisation demanding fee levels higher than the market average?

3 **Nurture your clients.** Attracting a new client is eleven times more costly than keeping an existing one. By investing in existing customer relationships, you are in effect increasing the effectiveness of your marketing and advertising by a factor of eleven.

4 **Nurture your centres of influence.** There are people in your network—they may not be your largest clients, or perhaps they are not clients at all—who have the ability and propensity to introduce and recommend you to your ideal clients. I call these individuals *Nexus clients*. Guarantee the bonds of your relationships with these Nexus clients and you are guaranteed to continually extend your lateral reach.

5 **Communicate with the market.** Don't expect immediate results. These are cumulative tactics, not single events. You cannot over-communicate with your market if the messages are value laden and able to be used by your prospective audience. Use the Marketing Whirlpool to communicate value in as many different ways and as often as possible.

6 **Ask for referrals.** Passive referrals are wonderful gifts but cannot be counted towards your marketing effort as a guide for future results. Because these referrals are passive, you cannot guarantee their continuance, or their size and number. You must take responsibility to ask for referrals. More about referrals in chapter 7.

7 **Run educational seminars.** Educating your clients generates many requests for additional help. Teaching your existing clients how they can achieve even greater

results—even without engaging your professional services—is a powerful and worthwhile endeavour. The more you teach, the more you learn. You will learn what issues your clients are currently facing, what they are most passionate about, their goals and aspirations, and how you can best be of service.

8 **Productise your smarts.** Create products to boost your brand and extend your reach. Creating products from your intellectual property is a nifty combination of passive income generated by active promotion. The products will enhance your credibility and help you reach new markets. The products can go to places much faster and more often than you ever could. These products will also help you generate additional business, and at times close the sale for you.

9 **Introduce and offer new and additional services.** The crux of lateral reach is to take your existing service offerings into expanded and new markets, while developing modified offerings and creating new offerings to present to your existing markets. Thinking in this expansive way allows you to extend your reach far beyond what is possible by marketing only existing services to new clients within your existing market.

10 **Publish case studies.** Publishing and disseminating case studies, whether in print or electronically, has been an enormous boon for many of my clients. I have written a thorough explanation of case studies in chapter 3.

11 **Become a person of interest.** I tell my clients, it's not so much how many people you know as how many want to get to know you. Are you the person that others actively seek out at business functions and events? Are you the person who people manoeuvre dining place cards so they can be seated next to at a business lunch? Gravitas is an attractive attribute.

12 **Be disciplined in Whirlpool Marketing.** Be tenacious and aggressively fuel the forces of attraction in your marketing. Success does not happen by accident, neither is it a single event. Dogged determination will drive your success.

Figure 5.2 shows an example of whirlpool activities that get stronger as you go deeper. At the top of the whirlpool you're making it easy and affordable for prospective clients to interact with you. As they begin to trust and respect you, the offerings become more valuable.

Figure 5.2: Whirlpool Marketing activities

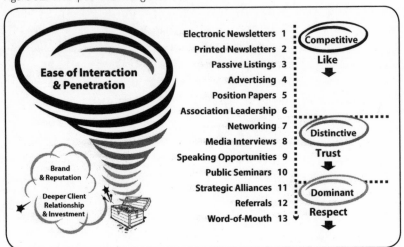

You Can't Make This Up

Harry Charalambous has been a close and valued friend since 1998. Harry has never been, and probably never will be, a client of mine. But he is a Nexus person within my community who has the remarkable quality of knowing everyone who is anyone in Brisbane. If there is someone I want to know, or if there is something I need, and I'm not sure of how to go about gaining access, Harry is the first person I will call. Nexus individuals like Harry can be the lifeblood of your business, in spite of not paying you a cent.

How to retain the client and their business

Many of you will empathise with those practitioners who doggedly work on building their firm, doing everything right, delivering quantifiable improvements to their clients, only to lose clients to the competition. You can establish great acquisition sources, but unless you back it up with post-purchase retention strategies you run the risk that someone else will eat your lunch.

While I was on a month-long business trip to the United States my wife had the kitchen gutted and remodelled. Before I left I wasn't aware it was going to happen, and by the time I returned from New York it looked as if the new kitchen had always been there. A job well done. Unfortunately, it was too well done, especially the lighting. The remodelled kitchen with elegant lighting drew attention to the relatively drab fixtures and fittings throughout the rest of the house. The electrician contracted by the builder for the kitchen project was unavailable. An alternate tradesman was contacted and an appointment made for him to call in to discuss the options. Arriving 30 minutes late, without apology, he and my wife got down to business as I worked my way down to the bottom of my martini glass. On the day it was arranged for him to install the new lighting (which necessitated that the mains power to the house be turned off) he was two hours late, which required him to work well into the evening. If we ever need electrical work again, I'll find another electrician.

In an episode of *The Simpsons*, Bart and Lisa are on an aeroplane and are upgraded to first class. Bart makes the comment, 'I come for the leg room, but I stay for the service'. Retaining your clients and sustaining your practice requires that you deliver exemplary customer service. It's no longer appreciated—it's expected. No matter how good your marketing is for acquiring new business, to retain your existing business your customer service must be outstanding. There is a customer revolution going on as people are becoming more aware of what they should be receiving by way of service and relationship. It doesn't matter whether you call your client a customer, a patron, a patient, a member, a sponsor or anything else, this point is sacrosanct: to be successful and happy in the future, you must guarantee that your clients are very happy as well.

Factors contributing to the retention of clients include:

* promptly returning telephone calls

* being respectful of appointment times and meeting these, always

- saying 'thank you'

- having fun with your clients, making sure your interactions are pleasant, even enjoyable

- offering professional administrative processes and payment options

- offering loyalty programs

- providing efficient and effective complaints handling

- seeking feedback from your clients

- listening to your clients and hearing what they say

- providing freely available resources on your website

- delivering unexpected communications (picking up the telephone just to say hello).

Customer service is about keeping it real and personal. Let your clients know how your organisation is faring, what you are improving, where you are doing well and what you are going to be doing next. Stay in touch with everyone you can, even if it's just to ask how they're doing. Always be courteous, polite and well-mannered, and display appreciation and selflessness. You will win over your clients by responding quickly to their requests in a way that demonstrates to them that you think they're important and you appreciate their business with you. Display confidence in your profession and your service offerings, have pride in your expertise, and do not apologise for or waver over your fees. Eliminate distractions that undermine your priorities and cause frustration for you and your staff. Treat your customers with the level of dignity, courtesy and respect you would demand for your own family, and you know that your service levels will always be on song.

CHAPTER 6

Develop market share without spending a fortune

It ain't braggin' if you can back it up.
**Dizzy Dean, Hall of Fame pitcher for the
St. Louis Cardinals**

Each time you engage with a prospect, a sale is going to be made. The question is: will you convince the prospect that you can help him or her, or will the prospect convince you that you can't? The sales process isn't adversarial. You're not out to conquer the client. The client and the professional are not on opposing sides.

In this chapter you learn how to:

- create the fundamental value proposition that differentiates you from your competitors

- reverse your thinking

- discover your value

- find fertile fishing waters.

There's nothing new under the sun. We all have got to where we are by standing on the shoulders of giants. It behooves us to position our value so it captures the attention of those we wish to attract and communicates why clients should choose us and not our competition. This is pivotal to our sales and commercial success.

Ric's Tip

We have to move from selling to audience attraction. Clients knocking on your door is better than you knocking on theirs.

Create the fundamental value proposition that differentiates you from your competitors

Why should I have to market when I'm an expert in my field?

Does your market really know what you do? Being an accountant doesn't mean you're the right type of accountant for every person or business. There are substantial differences between financial planners and investment advisers; commercial and litigation lawyers; patent attorneys and intellectual property lawyers. A fundamental value proposition creates an intellectual and emotional connection between you and your prospective client. It needs to be short, sharp and convincing.

When you articulate your value to a prospective client clearly and concisely so they comprehend specifically what you will do for them, you significantly improve your odds of winning their business.

These are the challenges:

- You have a broad range of service offerings that are in many ways complex and all-encompassing, and require a complete explanation. These services are very different from your competitors', and this difference must be explained so clients appreciate why you offer the better option. All of this takes longer than 30 seconds.

- It's easy to speak about what you do—just not in 30 seconds.

- Every prospective client is different. Recognising and conveying what will resonate with each can be difficult— and almost impossible in just 30 seconds.

- You tailor your solutions to each individual client's particular needs, objectives and circumstances. You can't explain something that precise in 30 seconds.

- You know what you do. Your clients know what you do. Your clients need you and want you. They're just unwilling to pay you what you're worth. You're perceived as a competitive commodity.

Articulating your value proposition will continue to be a hard sell, unless you define it as a client outcome.

'What do you do?' It's a straightforward question, and yet it is the bane of most professional service providers. Usually the professional will talk so much that they give the prospective client every opportunity to deselect them. Alternatively the professional will stammer and stutter and fall all over their words, appearing awkward and incompetent. What's needed is a successful value proposition that can be conveyed in what appears to be a spontaneous and conversational manner.

Even the most brilliant and experienced professionals can struggle with communicating a fundamental value proposition that sells. Being an expert in your field doesn't necessarily translate into being an expert at selling your services. We can find a myriad ways to mishandle selling ourselves. Here's a few that I've been guilty of and witness to:

- talking too much and boring prospective clients to death

- trying to be all things to all people (and therefore a master of none)

- saying an awful lot about nothing

- stuttering and spluttering, failing to explain the value

- being witty when what's really needed is to be professional

- giving the scripted sound bite of a late-night shopping channel host selling overpriced saucepans

- using reverse psychology—downplaying the value and expertise involved, hoping prospective clients will be intrigued.

Reverse your thinking

People don't buy tax returns. We do them only because it's the law. People do buy taxation compliance and, probably more to the point, taxation minimisation.

Enterprises don't buy audits. They buy an auditor's expertise. Why? So they comply with the *Corporations Act* and other statutory laws, and to obtain third-party validation that the financial representations made are correct and accurate.

People don't buy recruitment. They hire the expertise, industry contacts and knowledge of a recruitment professional to help them find a qualified individual who has the cultural fit to join the ranks of their existing team and deliver results to improve the business.

People don't buy a financial plan. They buy the strategies to protect their assets, increase net wealth, reduce tax and improve income.

Think more about what your client needs rather than the service methodologies you offer. Prospective clients don't necessarily understand the process of what you 'do', but they'll definitely comprehend how fixing their problems, reducing their pain or improving their bottom line will help. Your clients are not buying your methodology—they're buying the outcomes.

Discover your value

Why do your clients need your services? Why is this important? To discover your value, as it is perceived by your customers, you need to step out of your role and into the buyer's position. Why do your clients buy from you? What are the outcomes and results your professional services deliver for your clients? Ignore the features of your service, the inputs and the tasks. Ascertain the real reasons why clients buy from you, and what they perceive as being your true value for them.

- Why do clients choose your firm rather than a competitor's?

- What is recognisably different about you?

- What benefits, results and/or outcomes do clients gain from working with you?

- How would you describe your services and the work you do to an eight-year-old?

From the Front Lines

'We had sent out 23 proposals to provide recruitment services and had not won a single project. Clearly we were doing something wrong as we had built reasonable rapport with all 23 prospects before sending a proposal. Our thinking was that we were being underpriced by competitors.

'Analysing the proposals we recognised that the content was heavily focused on the process of what we would do in the recruitment project. We weren't differentiating ourselves and although we quoted our principles of quality and value, our proposals showed us as being a commodity. It was all process-driven.

'The clients could compare our services with other recruiters and we would all appear to be the same. The choice was being made on price. As one of our newer consultants commented, the clients probably got no sense of how we were worth the fee and were disinterested by the sameness of the proposal.

'We hired a temporary receptionist for a day, our entire staff huddled in the boardroom and we reversed our thinking. We asked and answered questions of ourselves like: What's it like working with us? What additional value does a client receive from us that they won't get elsewhere? Do they recognise this value? Can they measure it? What annoys clients about other recruitment firms? This is when we realised we were employment and HR consultants not just recruiters. We actually contribute to the organisational success of our clients.

'We immediately changed the way we thought about ourselves and spoke of our value to clients in our meetings with them and in our proposals. We won our next 7 proposals on the run and are now averaging 70–85 per cent success on proposals sent.'

—Brandon Lyle, Lyle Recruitment

Prospective clients must be able to see why you offer a better alternative than all the other available options. Do you know why you're the best option? If you can't articulate it, the marketplace will never appreciate and understand why they need you. Not only must you have a worthwhile fundamental value proposition, but you must be able to substantiate its claim. You have to be believable. It's a matter of trust. Trust is a matter of perception by your clients and your target audience. The value proposition should resonate with potential buyers of your services and immediately differentiate you from your competitors in some way. Then you must be able to convince those buyers of what you can do by substantiating your claims.

To resonate you must address the wants and needs of your buyers. You need to be certain of who wants what you can offer and is willing to pay for it. It's not your time, processes or methodology they're purchasing. It's their peace of mind: an increase in their revenues, performance and profits; and a decrease in their costs, production losses and inefficiencies. Buyers care about the performance of their own business, not yours.

It's vital that you convincingly iterate a measure of differentiation that allows you to stand out from the crowd and not be easily compared with your competitors. If not, you will be assessed and treated like a commodity, and a commodity is nearly always compared on price and price alone. The most enviable position from which you may differentiate yourself from others is at the relationship level. The relationship is the intangible non-purchase and can rarely if ever be compared. Customer service, offered as the differentiating factor by many services firms, initially may seem the most viable factor. Customer service, being the intangible purchase (that is, the standardised customer service you *must* provide because the client has bought from you), can be an opportunity for services firms to differentiate from competitors who may be on an equal footing in terms of expertise, experience, resources and so on. Any level of customer service you create that is distinct today, however, can be imitated and become competitive tomorrow. You will know that you've found a genuine point of difference when buyers cannot readily find a substitute for what you're providing.

Your ability to substantiate your fundamental value proposition is key to its success. It's not enough to be good—you have to know why you're good, and explain this to your target buyer audience. Prospective clients may want what you're selling, and may even perceive you to be the only source available for what they require. However, if they don't believe you can deliver on what you say, they will be unwilling to risk investing in you and your service. You not only need to walk the talk, but you also must talk it up.

Substantiating your value proposition requires you to have testimonials from buyers of your services. You can also back it up with case studies that demonstrate your knowledge and the successes your clients have achieved by implementing your advice.

A fundamental value proposition checklist

• Explicitly state who your preferred buyer or market is.

• Focus on the wants, problems and needs of the buyer.

• Describe the value of solving the wants, problems and needs of the buyer in their language, not yours.

• Demonstrate that you comprehend how to solve the buyer's wants, problems and needs.

• Establish the reasons why you are the preferred choice of service provider to do this type of work for the buyer.

It's not necessary that you have a single value proposition statement, because one size does not fit all. It is necessary to have the intelligence and smarts to adeptly and quickly move to what's required given the environment you find yourself in, and the types of people you are speaking with at that moment.

Finding fertile fishing waters

As a professional practitioner the best way to sell your ability to help is to help.

Fishermen tend to revisit the waters where they've had the most success. That's why so many professional practitioners tend to rely unconsciously on one or two types of marketing. Human nature, being what it is, influences us to market for new business and clients through previously charted waters where there was the least resistance. If we acquire a few new clients by attending Rotary Club meetings, we choose to attend those meetings in favour of any others that may conflict. If we attract a couple of new clients by advertising in a particular business magazine, we continue to advertise in that magazine even if client acquisitions have waned. Consciously or unconsciously, we focus our marketing efforts in areas where client acquisition has been easy and/or rapid, even if those results were not long-lived. Unbeknown to us, however, just over that nearby sandbar is a fertile fishing hole teeming with many more, much larger fish.

On the surface, it makes sense to continue our marketing in areas that previously have provided us with good results. As professional practitioners we aren't all natural-born marketers, so when we do hook a few it's common sense to keep using the same tackle and bait, and to visit the same fishing hole. It's the easy option, but it's not the only one. Just because strategic alliances brought in new business, it does not follow that all we should do is seek out more strategic alliances. Previous networking successes do not dictate that we focus solely on more networking. To create stronger growth it's incumbent on us to examine additional, new and disparate business acquisition sources. And there's strong evidence to support this type of new business exploration.

Marketing and business development is not a zero–sum process. Marketing actions are not mutually exclusive; we can continue with existing tactics while launching new and additional activities. Develop multiple activities to drive your Marketing Whirlpool (see figure 6.1). Initial marketing efforts should focus on activities with ease of client interaction and ease of market penetration to provide you with the quickest results. These include branding, sponsorships, networking, actively requesting referrals, and informal and formal strategic alliances. The more you engage in these Whirlpool Marketing activities the more disparate, additional and new business you will acquire.

Figure 6.1: Marketing Momentum: multiple activities drive further business

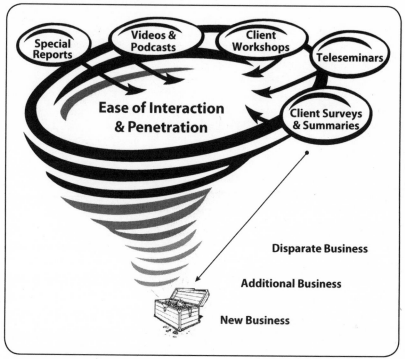

All marketing has a cost, even if it is only the time needed to implement it. All marketing has appended risk (see figure 6.2, overleaf), even if it is only a temporary loss of enthusiasm after a marketing piece fails. When one component of our marketing is successful, not only can we continue with that activity, but we can now afford to invest time, money, resources and intellect into an additional marketing activity. Existing successes fund new business acquisition adventures. I've termed this the Sequential Sigmoid Factor.

Figure 6.2: success correlated with time, revenue and risk

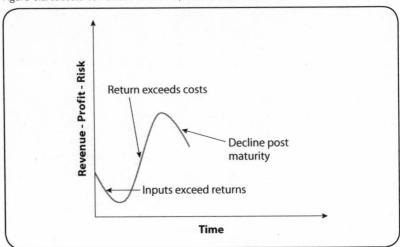

The Sequential Sigmoid Factor (see figure 6.3) describes how when the return on investment exceeds the costs of implementation, thus providing success, resources (time, revenues, people, capacity) become available to implement an additional or new initiative. It also allows for a higher level of tolerance of risk due to the insurance provided by the previous initiative's ongoing success. Failure to continually implement new and additional initiatives, and accept increasing levels of risk on the back of preceding successes, breeds complacency and laziness, which can be the undoing of a professional practice. As in any great whirlpool, breadth, depth and momentum are the keys to a powerful vortex.

The following suggestions for finding fertile fishing waters will already be known to many professional practitioners. My guess, however, is there isn't a single practitioner who is consistently and conscientiously using all of these lures, and there's no compulsion to use every single one. The challenge is to select three to five of these opportunities that you have yet to implement, and include them in your whirlpool to attract new and additional sources of business revenue.

Figure 6.3: Sequential Sigmoid Factor: self-funding for future growth and advancement

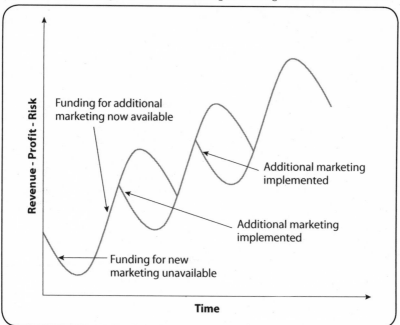

Some of the best marketing activities are:

1   forming strategic alliances

2   focusing on how small fish are sweet

3   publishing informative articles

4   becoming memorable for all the right reasons

5   joining professional and trade associations

6   creating a Referral Whirlpool

7   engaging in thought leadership

8   being an expert who speaks

9   reactivating clients

10   becoming a person of interest.

1 Forming strategic alliances

Formal and informal alliances are a powerful way to enable organisations to refer business to each other. Alliances work particularly well when there are common needs across the respective client databases.

Alliances need to be planned, driven and worked. New business opportunities from alliances won't just happen; you have to make them happen. Results will occur because both parties to the agreement are committed to making the relationship work. Partnerships like this are not just about sales; they can help to grow your business through partnering in activities such as seminars, workshops, events, newsletters, articles and promotions.

In any alliance it's important that:

- it makes sense to both businesses

- the business offerings are non–competitive

- the quality of product, service and relationship is comparable

- the professionalism of both businesses is comparable

- the respect you have for each other, your clients and your work is similar

- there is an exit clause for the alliance (if it is a formal one)

- remuneration, rewards or other types of compensation provided for referrals between your organisations are disclosed, transparent, and commercially fair and reasonable.

Select with whom you wish to create an alliance and the reasons for choosing that organisation. Enter any strategic alliance with your eyes wide open, your expectations of each other clear and the understanding that, just as with any other facet of your business, it needs to be part of your overall strategy. Finally, remember that it needs to be actioned to produce results.

Whirlpool Wisdom

'When our firm can give a client a service through a strategic alliance that might not have been available without it, then we have done what we set out to do—we have met a client's need and we have guaranteed our firm retains the client's trust and business.'

—Jesse Yvanoff, Principal of CJ Advisory

Whirlpool action: Make a list of 10 professional firms you have done business with or know well. With each firm make an appointment to meet the owner, principal or partner who has decision-making authority and personally knows you. The purpose of your meeting is to explore why and how it makes sense for your organisations to recommend clients to each other, and whether to make it a formal or informal alliance partnership. If you received only two new clients from each alliance partner in a year, it would still mean 20 new clients. That's significant for any business.

2 Focusing on how small fish are sweet

Sometimes we're overly ambitious in seeking only the trophy fish, those elusive prize catches that look stunning stuffed and mounted on the wall in our den. There's a reason why you notice a multitude of boats anchored in close proximity: the fish are biting, there's plenty for everyone, and although they're not trophy fish they make good eating.

- Who are regular buyers of services you have to offer?

- How might you chunk down your services to offer smaller options?

- How could you productise your services into stand-alone modules or components?

If you're a financial adviser you have more options than simply writing a full financial plan. You can, for example, provide a cash-flow analysis, a debt reduction plan, a personal taxation review or a retirement strategy. All of these smaller components can be offered for a lower investment by the customer.

If you're an accountant, auditor, lawyer, recruiter or consultant, there are countless ways to package up your smarts and offer them to the marketplace.

Whirlpool action: Deconstruct what it is you do into the smallest components that still make sense when they stand alone. What you're doing is unbundling your smarts. Package them into products that are easy to explain so that buyers will understand and value them. Next, list who wants each of those bundles, who is willing to pay for it and what they will get from it. Make a plan to duchess those potential buyers.

3 Publishing informative articles

Professionals seem reluctant to use publishing as a vehicle for promotion and branding. The reasons for that reluctance include a failure to accept the value of being published, a perception they are incapable of writing well, a mistaken belief that they don't have enough time, and an unwillingness to think about where to publish, who to contact and what to write about. Of those who do, a not-so-insignificant number shamelessly sell their services rather than providing valuable content and usable information. Self-promotional articles are boring to read, fail to enthuse the editor or reader, and do not inspire people to take action and reach out.

Writing informative, non-promotional articles full of worthwhile content is all the promoting you need to do. Publications provide a resources box or bio line that includes at least the author's name and website. Articles that include factual, objective and usable information without the sales pitches are much more likely to be accepted by the editor and get published. An even more powerful channel as you dive deeper into Whirlpool Marketing is the published interview in which you are the subject. *HR Agenda* is a bilingual human resources magazine published by the Japan

HR Society. The managing editor, Jun Kabigting, came to Kuala Lumpur to attend the inaugural Global HR Excellence Conference in 2012, where I delivered a full-day program to the entire delegation on the third and final day. After the conference Jun approached me for an interview. The magazine published a two-page spread about me and my thoughts on human resources, and promoted one of my books and my coaching program.

When you freely give tremendous value to the editor and reader, you're likely to receive much more latitude for subtle promotion.

Whirlpool action: List 12 publications you would like to target because their readers are your potential buyers. Obtain the editorial guidelines to learn if they will accept unsolicited articles and on what basis. Quickly browse through three editions of each publication to determine the tone of the articles they print. Approach one publication every week requesting their permission to submit a non-promotional article or with an offer to be interviewed. Your objective should be to have an article or interview published each quarter.

4 Becoming memorable for all the right reasons

The Kardashians may be memorable, but there is no substance or value supporting their fame. Perhaps in the world of entertainment, where one can become famous simply for being famous, that can work, but in business there has to be an engine under the hood. Every Apple store around the world looks almost identical: the clean white decor, bright lights and open space and staff in blue t-shirts. Apple stores are memorable for their consistency and back it up with products that perform amazingly well. Richard Branson and his Virgin Airlines are memorable for being fun, fast and funky while providing quality that is comparable to their competition's.

You can evoke similar strong responses by generating awareness of your business and what you offer, ensuring your marketing is of consistent high quality and is targeted appropriately for your audience. Exemplify excellence in everything you do, including your advice, marketing, work, products, staff, offices and behaviour. Your Marketing Whirlpool will pull clients towards you when you give them a reason. What aspects of your firm can you promote that are attractive to the audiences you most want to target? What is it about your work, service, knowledge, success and experience that will make people reach out to you? Focus on what it is you do best and how you deliver that to your clients.

There must be a stickiness to your marketing and branding for the market to remember you — no one ever got fired for buying IBM.

Whirlpool action: Select six of your most loyal high-quality clients. Individually, invite them to coffee, letting them know all you are seeking is their best advice and honest answers to three questions:

1   Why did you choose to engage us to do your work?

2   What do you like most about us and the work we do?

3   When you tell others about us, what do you say?

The answers to these questions will help you to develop a memorable brand.

5 Joining professional and trade associations

Professional and trade associations provide many opportunities to get noticed by prospective buyers, influencers, recommenders and partners. If you are ineligible to be a full member of an association to which your potential buyers belong, you may still be able to register for associate membership. So you can effectively manage your time and marketing effort, and target only the professional and trade associations where your potential buyers are members. Being a member of the association your audience belongs to helps you to understand and learn what's important to them, because this is what will be spoken about at most of the meetings and events. You will also be seen, by dint of your membership, as one of them rather than an outsider. Your involvement in meetings and activities will make it easier to initiate conversations with potential clients.

Create a Marketing Whirlpool for your involvement in professional and trade associations. Whirlpool activities may include (but not be limited to):

• speaking opportunities

• writing articles for the association's newsletter or magazine

- advertising with the association

- attending functions and events held by the association where you will be able to network

- taking a leadership position on the association's committee or board

- sponsoring an event run by the association

- networking at regular association meetings

- providing pro bono professional advice to the association (not to individual members)

- investing in a stand/stall to promote your services at association conferences or major events.

Whirlpool action: Identify five associations that you believe will position you to access potential buyers, influencers and recommenders of your services, and investigate the viability of gaining either full or associate membership. Ascertain the likelihood of being eligible to take a committee or board position. Investigate what type of newsletter or magazine the association produces and the production quality of that organ. Analyse the overall potential of being a member and whether you genuinely believe it will yield results over the next two to three years. Prioritise and select the best one or two with which to become involved (quality over quantity).

6 Creating a Referral Whirlpool

Referrals are the coinage of my realm. Starting from a zero base in 2004, I've built a significant international consulting base, all of which was created through referrals, recommendation, introductions and the like. Not one cold-call—ever! Referral business is the middle ground between cold-calling and having clients approach you because they have heard you're good and have already decided they need you. Everyone agrees that referral business is great business. That said, in all of my consulting and coaching work I repeatedly learn that people are not getting the quality referrals they want. In November 2011 the Society for

Executive Wisdom undertook a global survey of business on the topic of referrals. The survey found that:

- 90 per cent of respondents considered referrals either important or extremely important

- 98 per cent considered referrals to be good business

- less than 19 per cent accounted for referrals in their sales budgets

- more than 70 per cent did not have a formalised referral system

- fewer than half of businesses educated their employees on how to request referrals

- 92 per cent of businesspeople provided referrals to other businesses, but more than one–third didn't receive referrals from others.

To gain referrals, you have to be referable; if you can't describe what you do as an outcome, it will always be difficult to receive referrals. Create a system to request and receive referrals continuously. Be clear about the profile and the characteristics of the type of business or individual to whom you wish to be referred. From this create a list of specific organisations and people. For people to be able to help you, you have to know exactly who you want to be referred to. Bring a laser-like focus to your referral requests; timing is everything, but understand it is the quality and not the quantity of referrals that will improve your business. Build momentum in your Referral Whirlpool by developing multiple referral sources and maintaining ongoing relationships with those sources. Institutionalise your referral process and take responsibility for referrals end to end. Think of how and why you have recommended and referred others. What can you learn from that?

Factors influencing the success and value of referrals include:

- who you ask

- how you ask

- when you ask.

Affirm and sustain a mindset that you're not asking for a favour when seeking referrals; you're doing a favour by assisting colleagues, peers and friends of your existing customers.

Whirlpool action: Make it a goal to ask for one referral to one specific person each working day. This tight focus will produce a superior quality of introduction. Educate your clients to expect to hear from you regularly, and that you will be seeking referrals, recommendations and introductions to specific people who they know you would like to get to know. Reciprocate and make referrals two-way traffic. You have to give to get.

7 Engaging in thought leadership

I've read varying opinions on what makes a thought leader, and most of it is rubbish. Thought leadership is a relatively imprecise term used far too often to describe what is simply marketing or branding. Your name is your ultimate brand, whereas being seen as a thought leader transcends content. Seth Godin is a thought leader whom I would listen to on nearly any subject because he is a terrific thinker. Social media marketers working off one-page websites are not thought leaders. You will recognise that you're achieving recognition as a thought leader when you're getting noticed, and achieving commercial and professional reach outside your inner circle of business.

These are common characteristics of recognised thought leaders:

- They are completely at ease with top people in any field and know other thought leaders.

- They have an A-class client list.

- They are sought out by other professionals and the media.

- They are cited by others to prove their points of view and contribute intellectual property to their field.

- They speak at conferences or events, sharing their intellectual property.

- Although controversial, they admit to their errors and continually evolve.

Whirlpool action: In addition to other facets of Whirlpool Marketing, develop a series of courses for clients; get on a local or state panel of experts in your area of expertise; conduct research or write a series of position papers, and issue press releases on your results; teach a course at a local college or university as a guest lecturer or adjunct professor.

8 Being an expert who speaks

Speaking is a fabulous and exceptionally efficient way to promote your expertise. Speaking gets you noticed and the cachet attached enhances your perceived credibility, thereby making you a person of interest. It causes people to remember who you are and what your business does. The more people see you speak and see your business name, the more successful and knowledgeable people think you are. It also provides prospective buyers with a sample of the value you offer in a non-threatening environment. You're not required to be an expert speaker, simply an expert on the topic about which you'll speak. The key is not to be overly self-promotional. Provide practical advice rather than abstract concepts, and support your opinions with relevant examples. Avoid boring your audience with sophisticated research, but if you have undertaken such research, let them know you will make it freely available to anyone who requests it from you.

You don't have to be a professional or seasoned speaker to make this Whirlpool Marketing activity work for your business. If you're willing to speak for free and deliver substantive content, you'll find that there are more opportunities available than you can handle. Being an expert who speaks is not about selling your wares but selling your knowledge. Speaking opportunities are not limited to business events. There are also radio interviews, audio recordings on blogs and websites, webinars and web-conferencing, teleconferences, learning and educational institutions, and much more to be considered.

Whirlpool action: List 12 potential speaking opportunities at associations, business groups, networking events and the like. These are readily identified because they have previously invited speakers. Naturally, you will select those organisations and events where your potential buyers are likely to be in attendance. Craft a letter introducing yourself, your topic and the value their guests will gain from listening to your presentation. The content of your presentation must be topical and highly relevant for the audience. Mail the 12 letters and make a follow-up telephone call within three to five days of posting. Making a follow-up telephone call will significantly increase the odds of your approach to speak being accepted.

9 Reactivating clients

As already mentioned, attracting a new client is eleven times more costly than keeping an existing one. By investing in existing customer relationships, you are in effect increasing the effectiveness of your marketing and advertising by eleven times. Whirlpool Marketing incorporates client reactivation parallel to new client acquisition—not one or the other, but both. There are various reasons for a client to choose to sever the working relationship with you. So long as the cause was not an irreversible error, client reactivation can be an effective way to generate new business. The approach is crucial. Understanding why customers have become inactive is critical to devising the best engagement and communication approach. To increase the chance of reactivation, assess the client's past activity and behavioural interactions with you. Why did these clients sever ties with your firm? Perhaps your services and products are predictable. What's your goal in reactivating them? Is there a different value proposition you can put to them? How can you make it easy for them to re-engage with you?

Whirlpool action: What you must do now is stand out from the crowd and become interesting, puissant, remarkable and potent in the eyes of your clients. Review clients lost over the past 12 months. Identify those who you believe would profit from new or additional value you've created to which they haven't yet been exposed. Craft a sincere and legitimate approach that includes a follow-up telephone call within three days of their receiving your letter. Set a goal of reaching out to one lost client each week.

10 Becoming a person of interest

You can generate new business by becoming someone others are drawn to spend time with because of what they receive by belonging to your community. Rather than charisma, being a person of interest is about authenticity and value. Persons of interest are recognisable by the way they stimulate the thinking of those around them. It means you have a broad knowledge across many topics and that your acumen enables you to contribute intelligently to a wide range of discussions. You're able to draw on interesting experiences over your lifetime and share them with people in a manner that has relevance to them and is not all about you.

Being a person of interest is built on the foundation that you know other interesting people. By offering to connect and introduce people within your network you automatically become a Nexus person. Being well read helps make you an interesting conversationalist, providing you with ideas and knowledge that is relevant in most social and business settings. Persons of interest are identified by their:

- reputation and common ground with others

- genuine value freely shared

- demonstrable interest in other people

- point of legitimate difference

- capacity to benefit the people in their community.

Whirlpool action: Set a monthly target to introduce into your network and sphere of influence one new person who is interesting, intelligent and ambitious. Read one non-business book every fortnight, remembering to be eclectic in your choices. Every week watch at least one show on the Discovery or History channel on cable TV.

No matter how successful we become, there are always additional activities we can implement to increase business and client acquisition. I've provided just 10 of my personal favourites that deliver a high-value return. How many of these are you actively pursuing right now?

Best Practices

Research conducted by the Society for Executive Wisdom of 341 buyers of professional services highlighted exactly what's wrong in marketing and selling professional services. The research indicates that many Professional Knowledge Firms (PKF) are poor planners with regard to marketing strategy. The data suggests that many rely on a single marketing tactic and most spend money on marketing activities that do not produce a return on investment. Most interestingly, 84 per cent of buyers chose their PKF (accountant, lawyer, financial adviser) based on recommendation and referral. Furthermore, 83 per cent of the 84 per cent of buyers received the recommendation and/or referral from another PKF. If the creation of alliance partnerships (either formal or informal) is not already in your Whirlpool Marketing strategy, you may be forgoing a world of opportunity.

Achieving a measure of success is not a free pass to absolving yourself from testing new waters. It affords you increased security and resources to go further out from shore, deeper than before, and even sail an angry sea in search of bigger fish. Achieving success allows you to invest in a bigger boat, and there is always a bigger boat.

You Can't Make this Up

Medieval map makers would draw a dragon at the edges of the 'known world' to indicate that any travellers would be entering unknown territories and did so at their own risk. The famous copper Lenox Globe (c. 1503–07) bears the phrase 'HC SVNT DRACONES' (Latin for 'Here are dragons') around the east coast of Asia. Many sailors and explorers took the advice literally and were either warned off venturing into these regions or did so believing they risked provoking the ire of the dragons and sea-monsters that lived there. For some brave people the dragon indicated opportunity and a gateway to wonderful lands to be discovered and explored.

Implement the whirlpool to automate your lead generation

Customer service is done to death. But it's not done well. Every single day I am exposed to opportunities for businesses to improve their results by delivering slightly better service. And the larger the organisation, the worse they appear to be at delivering on this simple component. Employees are cogs in the wheel with no affiliation to the company, product or customer. It's a job that pays the bills and that's all. And it shows in their expressions, their language and their actions. Management are nowhere to be seen, preferring to hide out in their offices reviewing inconsequential and poorly actioned 360-degree feedback forms.

The feedback from my clients practising in accounting and law is that overwhelmingly they believe they must significantly increase lead generation and marketing efforts just to survive and maintain current levels of revenue. For 327 accounting practices surveyed by the Society for Executive Wisdom in the Asia–Pacific region in January 2013, new business growth was self-assessed to be their highest strategic priority (see figure 6.4).

Figure 6.4: self-assessment of strategic priorities

What this is telling us is that your competitors are chasing your clients, your prospects, your marketplace. But when business is tough for you, be assured that it is tough for your competitors too. Resist wallowing in self-pity. There's no point blaming the economy, the government, currency fluctuations, exchange rates, outsourcing. It's a trigger that you must continue to market, only better. Invest further in your Whirlpool Marketing. New business growth (business development, client attraction and acquisition, marketing, networking, referrals) is rated as the number one strategic priority. Therefore, you must become an 'ADDICT' to protecting and growing your business:

Assess: Review and benchmark your organisation against the best in your marketplace in terms of marketing, promotional tactics, networking and word-of-mouth.

Defend: Protect your existing clients through exceptional customer service and building long-term relationships for your mutual benefit.

Demonstrate: Demonstrate your competencies and expertise in ways that allow buyers to assess whether you're the best professional to help them with their needs. Create intellectual property and disseminate this to your target audience.

Initiate: Implement ideas that you've been considering for some time but just haven't got around to. Organisations often know what it is that they should be doing but procrastinate or defer implementation, claiming they're too busy for such matters. If you fail to attract new business and retain your existing business, pretty soon you won't be busy at all.

Communicate: When and how are you staying in touch with your prospective buyers? In a world of noise, where it's easy and inexpensive to blast the ether with emails, you must communicate in an effective and considered manner that is conducive to the needs and personality of those buyers you wish to engage. One size does not fit all.

Today: The competition is already speaking with your clients and your prospective clients. You can't wait until tomorrow, when you think you'll have everything just right. Set your strategy, design the action steps and get going. Do it today before you find someone else has eaten your lunch.

CHAPTER 7

Ensure repeat business, recommendations and referrals

Pay every debt, as if God wrote the bill.
Ralph Waldo Emerson

As professionals, we should engage with a new prospect determined to discover how we will quickly and effectively help that prospect achieve their desired results. This helps build your esteem and reputation in the eyes of the client and affords you every opportunity to win repeat business, recommendations and referrals. To guarantee this happens you need to think of how this client relationship will develop after five or more engagements. It's not only about this client wanting this work today, but about where you both may be professionally in the future. Your major clients will invariably stem from relatively few sources. Any truly new business from new sources should then always be treated as long-term business rather than as a short-term project.

In this chapter you learn how to:

- think ahead and plan for the fifth, sixth and seventh sale

- cement relationships that generate further sales

- get a referral every time

- attract quality referrals to keep your pipeline full

- implement the Referral Whirlpool.

Just asking for a referral is not good enough. Referrals are more likely when the product or service you deliver is sensational. Referrals and recommendations have built my business. Almost everyone in professional services will agree that referral business is great business. The cost of acquisition is low, resistance to meeting is reduced and sometimes even nullified, and the buyer usually has a positive inclination towards you by dint of the recommendation. The self-proclaimed business gurus tell us that we should request referrals as soon as we make the sale or gain the new piece of business, and sometimes even if we don't win the business we 'should still ask for a referral'. Nonsense! These approaches are not only flawed; they more than likely will jeopardise any future relationship with that client. Straight out asking for referrals makes everyone uncomfortable. They may promise to think about it and get back to you, but this is just a smokescreen to politely make you drop the subject and move on.

A genuine and valuable referral is earned, not requested. You earn referrals by providing sensational service; making yourself accessible and easy for people to do business with; consistently providing value to clients; and developing strong, loyal relationships with your clients. It's important that you remember to give in order to get. Be the exemplar for your clients and proactively give referrals where possible and appropriate. Don't wait to be asked... offer them regularly.

Think ahead and plan for the fifth, sixth and seventh sale

How often do you speak with your existing clients and discuss new competencies and capabilities you have acquired that they might need and could use? How often do you actively promote existing competencies and capabilities to a client who has yet to purchase those skills from you? A common failing by professionals of all types is that we assume the marketplace knows about all the service offerings we can provide. We wrongly believe that they know as much about our business as we do.

As I reach the end of my thirteenth year as a self-employed independent consultant, I am able to trace the origins of new projects this year to people known during previous years. The services I provide as an OD consultant will always be competitive with those of other highly skilled and educated service providers. My dominance in Australian and Asian markets has been achieved through my diligence in delivering breakthrough customer service and relationship. Nearly 85 per cent of my new business has originated from referrals, recommendations, introductions and word-of-mouth. This has not happened by accident. You can ensure repeat business for your practice by laying the foundations in the relationships you develop with your quality, ideal clients.

Not enough professionals respect the treasure chest lying on the sea floor awaiting their Marketing Whirlpool. The riches made available by thinking ahead and planning for future sales with existing clients include:

- prior business that hasn't been sufficiently investigated and appropriately explored (and ethically exploited). Let me be clear, it's not about closing sales or punching out proposals for newly created projects. Your purpose for staying in close contact and maintaining communications with previous and existing clients is to nurture your relationships, maintain the high level of mutual trust, and be uppermost in the client's mind when need and/or opportunity presents itself.

- individuals as your buyers, not the organisations they work for. Your relationships should be built with the people. When they move on, you move with them, and now you have a new client organisation. Reach out laterally and ensure that you build relationships with other key people around your buyer, so that when that person does move on, you will probably already know their replacement (or at least know the key people who will introduce you and recommend you to their replacement).

From the Front Lines

'Our strategies for the practice were inconsistent and ill conceived. Marketing was ad hoc and usually reactive. I hate to admit it, but it's true. We turned up to the office every day and got to work being industrial relations experts. In hindsight, we now know how much time was wasted with less than ideal clients. We were overworked, but it was all "in the business" not "on the business". In the 2½ years we've been using the Whirlpool Marketing System, our pipeline of clients has almost doubled, our practice is significantly larger, and we're much more efficient. Best of all, everyone in our practice now has time for family, holidays, and community volunteer work.'

—Gavin Neville, Partner, Workplace Wisdom

The keys to cementing relationships that generate further sales

While it may be helpful in some industries, adding nicotine or caffeine to the fees we charge will do nothing to enhance the client's dependency on you and your firm. Only one ingredient will do that, and it's not on any pharmaceutical or prohibited goods list. It is, quite simply, sensational customer service. How does your practice perform at consistently delivering client service that is sensational? If you're in accounting or law, client service is immediately disadvantaged and—whether you realise it or not—there are obstacles discouraging you from providing the level of service that you know would give you a competitive advantage. From your very first day on the job, you were handed a timesheet full of neat little boxes, each of which, when ticked, added another six-minute increment to a client file. The office manager explained to you that you must accrue enough of those neat little ticked boxes to accumulate a minimum of eight billable hours every day.

As an example, let's analyse how customer service is hindered by everyday machinations in a CPA or chartered accounting firm. You may not be an accountant, but most of us in professional services will fall prey to some if not all of these issues:

- Accountants are educated to be accountants, not customer service personnel. Being technically brilliant is vital, but so are excellent customer relations. If your clients do not feel they are listened to and appreciated, no emotional connection will be made.

- Accounting professionals have little client contact early in their career. Mostly, it's only after they are fully qualified with the CPA or CA designation that personal meetings with clients commence. It's at this point that they are suddenly expected to develop relationships and acquire new business. New business expectations dramatically increase as the professional becomes an associate director, director, salaried partner and then equity partner. But nowhere during this transition has there been any formalised education in customer service and relationship.

- The billable hour is so revered that non–billable activity is discouraged and denigrated. The accounting professional has learned—from the behaviour exemplified by others in the firm—to forgo client service and relationship activity in preference to ticking another hour billed.

- Most accounting practices charge fees in the most unimaginative way—hourly rates. This approach is ineffective, inefficient and unethical, and repeatedly undervalues the benefit to the client from the services provided. Value-based fees, project fees, retainers and the like are much more appropriate, efficient and ethical.

- Clients care only about their business, not the accountant's. The objective of the client is to complete the regulatory requirements, maximise their incomings and minimise their outgoings. If accounting professionals articulated the value of the services they provide in terms of client outcomes and results, clients would happily pay the fees commensurate with that. Clients are not paying you for your time; they are paying you for the benefits you produce for them.

Ric's Tip

As professionals we need to move from service-marketing to audience-marketing.

Why is customer service and client relationship so vital to professional services practice? Isn't the reality that clients simply want the best available professional, and the bedside manner is of no real consequence? How can you be sure that you will always be the best, technically? How can you be certain that you will always communicate to your marketplace how and why you're the best, and be believed? If you're a criminal lawyer you can spend hundreds of thousands of dollars on marketing, but until someone gets charged with a crime, they're not engaging your services. No matter how technically good a financial planner, or recruiter, or business coach may be, their expertise has to be in demand by someone before they will be hired. Regardless of how good and how often you market, you have to wait for the need to arise before you have the chance to provide your professional solution.

So professional services providers need to be remembered and easily contactable at the precise time a buyer perceives a need. Your marketing, therefore, must focus on frequency and recency, and you must remain in the front of their mind until the need arises. Marketing does matter and it needs to create the situation in which you are the preferred option in the mind of your prospects at the precise time they recognise the need. In a competitive field it's not being 100 times better than your competition in any one facet of your business that will guarantee you a competitive advantage. Rather, being just a little bit better in 100 different facets will give you the competitive advantage that attracts, influences and retains clients.

Ric's Tip

The horse that runs first wins 10 times the purse of the second-placed mount. But the horse does not need to be 10 times better — it only needs to win by a nose.

A team of statisticians studied two thoroughbred racehorses that competed in the same races over an entire season. One horse accumulated over $1 million in prize money for the season, the other only $50 000. That's a 20 to 1 ratio. Interestingly, when the race times of the two horses were compared, the horse that earned

20 times the prize money was only an average 3 per cent faster. A 3 per cent differential converted to a $950 000 advantage. The second horse that accumulated only $50 000 in winnings was still 97 per cent as good when compared by race times.

Malcolm Gladwell highlighted the anomalous results of reward in relation to effort in his book *The Tipping Point*. Mediocre effort produces minimal results, at best. Consistently greater efforts will produce some improvement in results attained. Paradoxically, it requires only a minimal increase in effort over your closest competitor to be rewarded significantly more than that competitor. This is known as the reward–effort paradox (see figure 7.1). To wear the green jacket you don't need to shoot four perfect rounds of golf. You just have to be one shot ahead of the next best player.

Figure 7.1: the reward–effort paradox

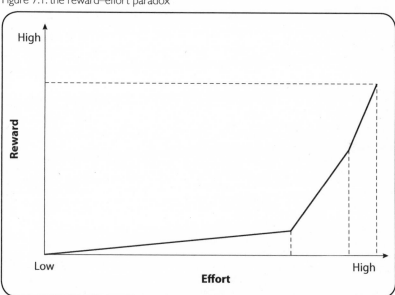

This is equally true for us in professional services. We need only win by a nose to achieve a significant advantage and amazing results. It's the practice that goes just one step deeper into the Marketing Whirlpool that discovers the treasure chest:

- one more published article per quarter
- client telephone calls returned five minutes faster

- one more networking event attended

- one more client–education event delivered

- one additional coffee meeting with a Nexus person per month.

If your practice continually moves 100 marketing elements forward an inch rather than one element forward a mile, you will win by a nose. Providing that little extra effort and value is all that is required to give you the edge over your competition.

To review the whirlpool basics, you begin by focusing on ease of client interaction and ease of market penetration. At this initial level you are competitive, even though liked. As you create more sophistication and marketing firepower you become distinctive, and clients learn to trust you. When your marketing is at its strongest your dominance in the marketplace commands the respect of your clients and prospects. At the deeper levels of the whirlpool your brand and reputation are at their best, and the client relationship and investment is deeper (see figure 7.2).

Figure 7.2: Whirlpool Marketing basics: win by a nose

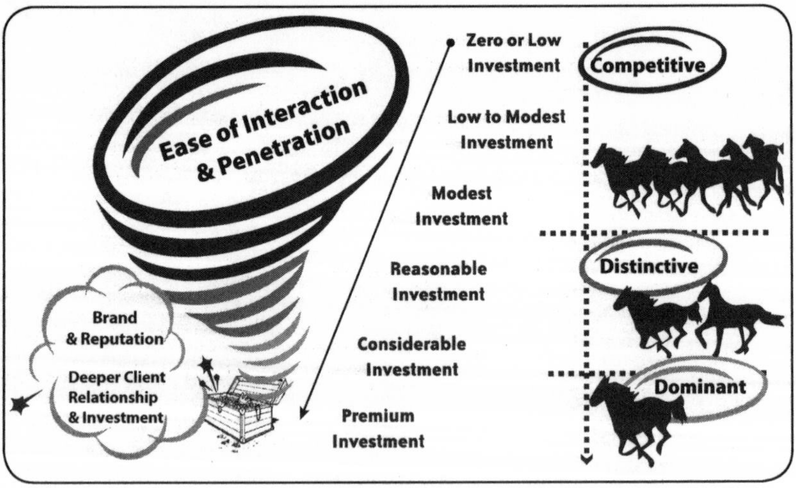

You Can't Make This Up

For my birthday, I received a gift voucher to a boutique bookstore in Bulimba, Queensland. The voucher is valid only for 12 months from the date of issue. Why? Will the books become relatively cheaper and thereby make my voucher more valuable? Does the voucher increase in value as time progresses? Is $200 in the bookstore's bank account now worth less to them when I exchange the voucher for merchandise two years from now? Explain to me why anyone who is serious about building customer relationships would consider it a positive branding exercise to place an expiry date on what is essentially cash. This single transaction upsets two customers: the purchaser of the voucher, and the recipient. When I'm forced to dance to the tune of another's fiddle, I'm not inclined to spend additional funds. This 'policy' can only annoy and upset. There's no upside whatsoever. It's easier to favour an organisation when the organisation favours you back.

How to get a referral every time

- Do you *deserve* to receive referrals?

- Do you *think* you deserve to receive referrals?

- Do you feel like a *salesperson* when you ask for referrals?

The first key is to be referable. Make it easy for others to refer and recommend you. You can assist others to refer you by clearly articulating what your value is. What impact do you have on your client's business? If you can't describe this as an outcome, it will always be hard to receive referrals. Reverse your thinking and explain how you solve the needs of your clients, rather than the service methodologies you offer. Stop thinking about your services, and start thinking about the client outcomes and results. To be referable you have to resonate with those people whom you want to recommend you. Promote your strongest asset—in client terms—and your single greatest point of differentiation. Do this in a way that is simple and straightforward so it can be easily remembered and repeated by everyone on your staff and by your clients. It's important to substantiate this in as many ways as you can, such as through client testimonials, published case studies and media exposure.

It is naïve to rely on accidental referrals. You need to be clear about specifically who you want to meet. You can then investigate who in your network knows the people able to introduce you to those you want to meet. The second key is to ask for referrals before you need them—don't wait until you're desperate. If you arrive at a place where you desperately need referrals, I can guarantee you will do it all wrong and the referrals will not come. Or, if you do receive referrals, the ones you get will most likely be wrong for you and your business.

We all feel good when we are able to help someone. Attract referrals by explaining to people that you need their help and ask, 'Who do you recommend?' As with any facet of life and business, mutually respectful and supportive relationships will have a greater propensity for success. If you're not actively seeking referrals while working with a customer, then perhaps you haven't convinced yourself of your own value. Otherwise, why would you not consider it your obligation to ensure others have access to you?

When clients come to you through referral or recommendation they are already attuned to you and your offerings. Your professionalism and credibility are supported and strengthened by the fact that their contact has put their reputation on the line by recommending you. The relationship with those who are referred to you commences on a foundation of value. Compare that with how your relationships begin with those whom you cold-call. How do you think you should be investing your marketing efforts and what strategies do you believe make best sense to propel your professional success? Do your marketing strategies make you a person of interest and someone who is easily referable?

Be confident in asking for referrals and get to the point. There's no shame in asking for referrals, because you know that your clients themselves seek them. Importantly, to make the act of seeking referrals successful you must always take responsibility for the next steps. Never second-guess yourself or your value in asking for referrals. When you build your business through referrals you have more available time to provide excellent attention to clients because you don't need to be prospecting for new business as much.

How to attract quality referrals to keep your pipeline full

At any stage in your career, whether as a veteran or a neophyte, there is a constant requirement to keep your pipeline full. Referrals and word-of-mouth are excellent tactics to adopt and implement to assist in achieving this objective. Every professional I speak with acknowledges and appreciates the significant value these two facets of marketing bring to any firm, but few have developed a system to continually acquire referrals.

It's worthwhile to understand why and how referrals and word-of-mouth work so well. According to the friendship paradox, a phenomenon first observed by the sociologist Scott L. Feld in 1991, on average most people have fewer friends than their friends have. The premise is that because your friends have more friends than you do, you can expand your community of friends by being in the company of your friends. Interestingly, research undertaken by Ezra Zuckerman and John Jost in 2001 contradicted this, finding that most people believe they have more friends than their friends have. People with more friends are more likely to be your friend in the first place; that is, they have a higher propensity to make friends. The implication of the friendship paradox is that the friends of randomly selected individuals are likely to have higher than average centrality.

The mathematics behind the friendship paradox explain the rationale for why referrals and recommendations are so good for business. The more you request and receive referrals, the greater the network from which you can avail yourself of even more referrals and recommendations: the whirlpool continues to deepen and strengthen. It's also evident that those people who are willing and able to refer and recommend you will be referring and recommending you to others with the same capacity. We tend to congregate in communities of people like ourselves, so if we are willing to recommend you, our friends will also.

10 steps to quality referrals

1   Develop relationships with other professional service providers who offer complementary services to your business, for the purpose of exchanging referrals. However, do this only with people you trust completely. Would you refer your best friend, your grandmother or your best client to this person and feel completely at ease?

2   Educate your clients to expect to hear from you regularly and that you will be seeking referrals, recommendations and introductions to specific people they know who you would like to get to know. Explain to your clients that you are able to provide them with such high levels of customer service because you are a referral-based business. As such, you're not required to market for new people as much as your competitors, which affords you the time to invest in your existing clients. By providing regular referrals, your clients are helping themselves by helping you.

3   Reciprocate and make referrals two-way traffic. You have to give to get, and if you give referrals to your clients when appropriate, they will be more inclined to do the same for you.

4   Consider vendors and suppliers as opportunities for referrals as well. Don't be shy to ask them for introductions to people with whom they do business.

5   Create your own networking events to make it easy for people to refer and recommend you. Host your own business breakfast or lunch, seminar or workshop on an industry topic, new research, regulatory or government changes, or industry trends, for example. Invite your clients, colleagues, friends and associates, and specifically tell them they are very

welcome to invite their own guests to bring with them to your event.

6 Word-of-mouth is a form of referral. Generate sensational word-of-mouth by being excellent at what you do. And gently remind your clients of how good you are. This gives them something to talk about with people they know.

7 Always thank those people who provide you with referrals, whether or not the person they referred does business with you. Communication is key to allowing people to feel comfortable about regularly referring people they know to you.

8 Put in place a formalised process of re-engaging and contacting all of your previous customers and clients. The reason for the contact is to ask them to introduce you to someone they know. These customers have done business with you in the past; it's only reasonable to expect that they know others who might like to do business with you too.

9 Always ask for testimonials. These can be in the form of a letter, an email, a video or an audio recording for your website, or even a recommendation on your LinkedIn or Facebook page.

10 Make the time to tell your clients about the other services you offer that they themselves may not yet have used. Frequently we assume that our clients know everything that we do. The reality is they probably only know about what you've done for them and think that is all you do.

Whirlpool Wisdom

Asking for referrals in a professional and forthright way will never hurt you or your business, but it could be the linchpin to leveraging substantial success. You will never be worse off by asking for introductions and recommendations. But if you don't ask, who knows what opportunities you will miss?

Use the Referral Whirlpool

Starting with the ubiquitous 'Who do you know…?' is an incredibly lazy way to ask for referrals. Instead, use the whirlpool approach (see figure 7.3):

• Ask your client if she can introduce you to other departments within her organisation.

• Ask your client for a referral to the industry associations and groups she belongs to.

• Ask your client to refer you to her suppliers.

• Ask that supplier to introduce you to his industry associations and groups.

• Ask the executives of these associations and groups if they can introduce you to key people in government departments they deal with.

• Word-of-mouth will begin working for you through all levels of the whirlpool.

Figure 7.3: example of Referral Whirlpool leverage

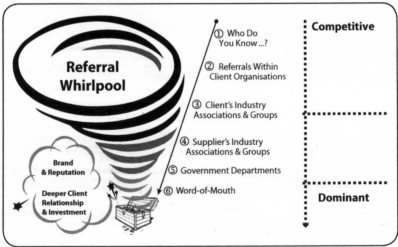

Ric's Tip

There are prospective clients everywhere you go. Never dumb down, talk down or dress down; you never know whose company you're in, and how they may directly influence your business.

Implementing the Referral Whirlpool will create amazing power, and fuel the centrifugal force that attracts new clients to you and your practice. Select six A-class clients and ask for three referrals from each of them over the next 12 months. That's only one referral every four months! Now you have an additional 18 quality people with whom you can start building relationships that may possibly lead some to engage your professional services, 18 people who as they get to know you will speak of you, refer to you and recommend you. The power of the whirlpool has just grown exponentially. Replicate this process with another six A-class clients and you are now producing enormous attraction to your whirlpool vortex!

Table 7.1 (overleaf) illustrates an accelerated plan. In January ask six A-class clients for one referral each. In February ask six different A-class clients for one referral each. In March ask another six A-class clients for one referral each, and in April ask a different six A-class clients. By the end of April you have asked 24 A-class clients for one referral each. That's 24 new introductions. In May, you start again with the original set of six and repeat the process. By the end of the year you've been referred to 72 new people from 24 A-class clients. (Change the numbers to suit your practice's client base demographics and numbers.)

Table 7.1: the power of the Referral Whirlpool

Month	6 A-class clients	6 A-class clients	6 A-class clients	6 A-class clients	Referrals received
Jan	1 each/ 6 total				6
Feb		1 each/ 6 total			6
Mar			1 each/ 6 total		6
Apr				1 each/ 6 total	6
May	1 each/ 6 total				6
Jun		1 each/ 6 total			6
Jul			1 each/ 6 total		6
Aug				1 each/ 6 total	6
Sep	1 each/ 6 total				6
Oct		1 each/ 6 total			6
Nov			1 each/ 6 total		6
Dec				1 each/ 6 total	6
Totals:					72

Research into referrals

In November 2011 I undertook to research referrals specifically with regard to professional services. The overview alone is telling. Of 336 respondents:

- 62 per cent were business owners or partners
- 90 per cent considered referrals important or extremely important

- 98 per cent considered referrals as good business

- fewer than 19 per cent accounted for referrals in their sales budgets

- 96 per cent admitted they'd prefer to receive more referrals

- more than 70 per cent did not have a formalised referral system

- fewer than half of organisations educated their employees on how to request referrals

- 92 per cent of businesspeople provided referrals to other businesses, but more than one-third didn't receive referrals from others.

This research, while not exhaustive, is indicative of the sentiment in the business world. The two main regions we researched were Australia and the United States, although Canada, Asia and Europe were also represented. The results showed that we actively and happily refer others. Consider this: you have probably many times recommended your doctor, your dentist, your lawyer or your accountant. You have never been uncomfortable doing this. You felt as if you were doing that person a favour by making others aware of how happy you are with your service providers. Why should it be any different when the roles are reversed? You do good work, you provide excellent return on investment to your clients, and your customer service is primo. Why would you believe that your clients would feel uncomfortable recommending you to their colleagues, peers and friends?

By proactively asking for referrals you are simply guaranteeing the process that would otherwise happen if the circumstance arose. You're no less important or valuable than the people you recommend.

Best Practices

Creating alliances with complementary businesses for the exchange of referrals makes good sense. However, only build referral alliances with businesses you're confident and comfortable will exhibit the same exemplary behaviours you maintain in your own business.

Summary of research results into referrals

How valuable do you consider referrals are to your business?
Some 70.9 per cent of businesses (74.5 per cent of Australian businesses) thought referrals were extremely important and valuable to their business, and an additional 19.5 per cent considered referrals highly important. That's a total of 90.4 per cent (94.1 per cent in Australia) who view referrals as highly or extremely valuable and important.

Do you have a formalised process to communicate with referral sources?
Sadly, however, 67.6 per cent (68.6 per cent in Australia) did not have a formalised process to communicate with referral sources to thank them and keep them apprised of the outcome of introductions.

What percentage of your current business revenues is the result of referrals?

- 1–9 per cent of total revenue estimated by 16 per cent of respondents

- 10–24 per cent of revenue estimated by nearly 27 per cent of respondents

- 25–49 per cent of revenue estimated by nearly 15.5 per cent of respondents

- 50–74 per cent of revenue estimated by 19 per cent of respondents

What's the problem with referrals?
We haven't educated our clients to appreciate the value to them of referrals as the foundation of our marketing. Have you ever been the recipient of poor customer service? Have you ever had to wait days, even weeks for your telephone calls or emails to be returned? Have you found it difficult to obtain information about a product or service you were interested in? Perhaps the reason is that the organisation is so busy chasing new business that they do not, or cannot, allocate enough time to these important areas of the business.

Where is the value in referrals?

Organisations that attract most of their business from referrals and recommendations are able to allocate sufficient time and resources to delivering exceptional customer service. This is why referral business is one of the best and most valuable ways to do business for both you and your clients.

What do you need to do to attract referrals?

If people aren't talking about you, it's probably because you're boring. Your marketing is boring. Your pricing is boring. Your message is boring. To get people talking about you, you have to be remarkable. When people are talking about you the opportunity for those people to refer you grows exponentially. In professional services, publicity stunts don't count. Most will hurt you rather than help you. To attract referrals you need to influence people into talking about you in a positive and grateful way. Develop a referral system that is incorporated into your customer relationship processes and marketing strategy. The referral system has to be pragmatic, valuable, useful and regular. The best referral is one that you do not have to ask for and that is a fit for your 'ideal client profile'.

The research results direct us towards some indisputable conclusions about business referrals:

- Everyone in professional services—from owners through to partners and managers, and even BDMs and salespeople—considers referrals extremely valuable to the business.

- Everyone considers referral business to be excellent business.

- Everyone would like to receive more referrals and be confident in doing so.

Unfortunately, even those people you would expect to be educated, experienced and confident in attracting and acquiring referrals are failing to achieve what they would like to. What's required is to develop a strategy and a process, supported by systems and actions, that will enable more referrals, from more people, of a high quality on a consistent basis. To be successful it will require discipline, tenacity, confidence and self-esteem. It's achievable, it's possible and it's simple.

What is the value of referrals influenced by?

The research showed some interesting factors with regard to the value of referrals. Factors influencing that value include: who you ask, what you ask for, how you ask, why you ask, when you ask, what your value proposition is and what the perceived value is to the client, and the referrer's value.

Who is not comfortable asking for referrals?

Professional service providers not comfortable asking for referrals include: 32 per cent of accountants, 11 per cent of banking professionals, 22.5 per cent of business coaches, 26 per cent of consultants, 20 per cent of finance industry people, 35 per cent of insurance professionals, 30 per cent of legal professionals, 66.5 per cent of professional speakers, 15 per cent of recruiters, 23 per cent of IT people and 25 per cent of business trainers.

What is the value of networking groups?

Networking groups are only as valuable as the members of the group. Many respondents expressed their dismay at how very few genuine referrals they received by attending weekly breakfasts as part of their business networking group. There was also despair at the poor quality of these referrals. Many declared that they believed they were giving far more to the group, for far too long, than they were receiving in return. Some had even grown to resent their membership of the group and had cancelled, failed to renew or were intending not to renew their membership.

What networking groups provide the best referrals?

There was no commonality in the research results from which you could assume a particular networking group guaranteed regular, quality referrals. Strategic alliances, however, did rate exceptionally well in the research results, which makes sense. When you create a strategic alliance, you do so specifically with another person or business because you like, trust and respect them, the work they do and the values they espouse. Strategic alliances are more specific and open in nature in that the referrals and recommendations are two-way traffic. My advice to clients over the years has been to create your own networking groups and invite specifically the people and organisations you want to participate. In this way you maintain control, you are seen as the leader and the central focus of the business group, and ultimately you become a Nexus person for the entire group. Success is therefore far more likely.

There's no argument that referral business is great business. And it's a way most of us would prefer to begin a relationship with a prospective customer. Professional services firms love referrals, yet most we spoke to admitted they feel uncomfortable and uncertain about asking for them. The research highlighted that people are not working effectively at making referrals a structured process, much as they would other important facets such as invoicing and proposal writing. Implementing a user-friendly, pragmatic system to attract and receive referrals will add a whole new dimension to your business.

Ric's Tip

One respondent explained that they included a 'referrals appreciated' blurb in their newsletters, on their website and on all printed marketing collateral.

If you are not comfortable asking for referrals, why is that?

Listed below are exact, unedited quotes from the responses received during our research and are listed in no particular order within each grouping.

Education

- I don't know the best way to ask — it would be great to have a few scripts that are proven.

- I'm not sure how to go about it, or who to ask. Unsure how to approach it.

- Lack of confidence.

- Don't have a formalised referral system.

- Sometimes too busy to do active campaigns, or too involved in daily work to dedicate time to this part of the business.

- Just feel awkward about asking.

- I think our sales guys are uncomfortable because they are afraid of getting a 'no' and the knock-on effect that would have on the relationship.

- I forget to ask until I've walked away.
- I don't have an effective process.
- Don't know how to do it professionally and with dignity.

Misunderstanding our own value

- If we did a good job referrals should just happen.
- It's not my usual thing to ask for referrals.
- Don't want to be seen to be touting for business.
- We find that the customer is happy with our service and asking for referrals appears to detract from that euphoria; you can see them say 'What is in it for me?'
- Don't want to appear pushy (but I have started to ask existing clients for them and it's been good so far).
- I find when I start asking others for referrals they run in the opposite direction. I try to give first and then referrals come.

Self-esteem

- Imposes a workload on someone you are trying to service.
- Sound desperate by asking.
- Seems too much of a strong-arm tactic.
- Don't know how to ask for referrals without feeling as if I am being a salesman and begging for help/business.
- I feel like it is begging for business—and if I'm successful I shouldn't have to.
- I am an introvert.
- Seems pushy, I would rather the recommendation was genuine from the heart.
- Do not want to constrain the existing relationship by 'appearing' pushy.
- Feel like it is an imposition.

Who is the best at referrals?

What became obvious from the results of this research was that most in professional services receive referrals accidentally. The percentages of professionals who do not have a formalised referral system was staggeringly high (73.6 per cent). The responses indicated that referral marketing is reactive almost to the point of passivity. This, of course, was at odds with the percentage of respondents who stated that they would like to receive more referrals (95.6 per cent).

So who doesn't have a structured and formalised referral system? The survey produced the following figures for respective professional groups: accountants (82.8 per cent), banking (72.7 per cent), business coaches (64.5 per cent), consultants (78.8 per cent), finance and financial services (60 per cent), health and medical (66.7 per cent), insurance and risk management (75 per cent), law (78.8 per cent), mortgage brokers (61.8 per cent), professional speakers (66.7 per cent), recruitment and HR (67.7 per cent), technology and IT (71.4 per cent), business training and facilitation (75 per cent).

BDMs and salespeople are good at referrals, aren't they?

The research produced some startling results on business development managers and salespeople:

- 14.7 per cent do *not* actively seek referrals

- 70.6 per cent do *not* have a formalised referral system

- 50 per cent do *not* record or measure referrals

- 41.2 per cent do *not* regularly receive referrals

- 81.3 per cent do *not* account for referrals in their sales budgets

- 60.6 per cent are *not* educated in attracting and requesting referrals.

What did the survey respondents believe to be the best way to get referrals?

It's no secret that referral business is good business—and yet it is the least utilised and most poorly implemented of the business development skills in professional services firms. What's peculiar is that everyone is more than happy to (and does) refer other professionals, frequently. Are you doing what's necessary to attract and receive regular referrals? The answers provided during our survey suggest that nearly all referrals that do happen occur by accident. They are received, not requested. How much opportunity is being squandered?

The accounting sector declared they rely heavily on satisfied clients telling other people, thereby providing unsolicited referrals. More than half of the accountants in the research stated this was their best source of referrals. A reasonable number declared their best source of referrals was from other professionals such as lawyers and financial planners. Word-of-mouth and friends also scored well.

The responses from those in banking, finance, financial services, insurance, risk management and mortgage broking were evenly spread. The majority of responses included: satisfied clients telling others about their services, referrals from other professionals (formal and informal), directly asking clients for referrals and networking and networking groups.

The array of answers from recruitment consultants was interesting and included: strategic alliances, word-of-mouth, other complementary professionals, asking existing clients and candidates, networking and networking groups, friends and offering incentives.

Some respondents were very clear that they received referrals from existing clients and others because of their professionalism, style and personal approach and the value for which they are recognised. Building a network of centres of influence was also a common thread among respondents. Many mentioned that they belonged to specific networking groups. The majority of those people also believed that the level of referral business they were attracting was far lower than would reasonably be expected. Just being a member of a 'referral association' does not open the floodgates. What was painfully clear is that a majority of respondents admitted that most referrals were unsolicited, unexpected and almost accidental. Therefore they were at a loss as to how to replicate their referrals success.

CHAPTER 8

Communication, influence, persuasion: customer centricity

People don't like to be sold, but they love to buy.
Jeffrey Gitomer

Consistency is valued. Inconsistency is commonly recognised as an undesirable personality trait. If your deeds don't match your words, which don't match your beliefs, people will judge you to be indecisive, confused or even hypocritical. One key to your success in acquiring new business is your ability to communicate persuasively. Effective communication helps you to influence and persuade. Clients have to understand the value of what you have to offer with the same clarity that you do.

In this chapter you learn how to:

- control the conversation by asking questions

- break mental barriers and get the client thinking your way

- understand the psychology of influence and why it's important

- build support and momentum for your work among others

- create a customer-centric culture.

Nobody likes being sold to, but nearly everyone loves a fantastic offer. If I invite you to join me in a corporate box at the Olympics, there's little to no resistance on your part. You either accept or decline. It's not incumbent upon me to identify your 'pain', find your 'hot button' or 'answer your objections'. Seth Godin explains that the sales assistant in the Apple store doesn't 'sell'. There's a line out the door on release days of new Apple products! The sales assistant simply offers you options regarding memory, colour and accessories. If you don't want it, 'Next, please'. This is one of the keys to Seth's amazing insights with regard to what he terms Permission Marketing.

If your marketing is superb, selling becomes a heck of a lot easier. Essentially, you offer options. The professional adviser who complains that she could win the business if only she could drop the fee is avoiding her job. The objective is for you to make it so easy for the client that essentially all they are doing is deciding on an option you've offered. The key to your success in reaching this point is your ability to communicate persuasively. Prospective clients have to understand the value of what you have to offer with the same intensity you do.

Effective communication is essential to any business that aspires to succeed, especially if targeting to increase its market share. When communicating, listener and speaker share an equal responsibility for making the message comprehensible; but communicating effectively goes far beyond the usual speech and hearing. You can't describe a speech as effective if it's not persuading or influencing the listener or the target audience in some way or another. The main aim of communication is to get things done the way you wish them to be done; simple as that. For businesses, communicating with clients is indispensable, and the main reason entities get in touch with customers is to get their product or services purchased. How do they achieve this successfully, though?

Let's also consider that we are constantly telling the marketplace what we are: the best accountant, the top specialist recruiter, the smartest lawyer, the most well-informed financial planner. That's easy to say. But what is it that you are not? Thinking in this counterintuitive way can help you better identify what it is you should be doing and inform your target audience what you will and won't do. Look at your advertising and identify what it is that you can remove. Eliminate everything you don't want to do. An awareness by you and your target market of what you won't do ensures you'll gain more time, experience less stress, and enjoy the work you do much more. The quality of work you produce will improve, as will your reputation; and the word-of-mouth, referrals and recommendations will come in much more quickly.

Ric's Tip

The meaning of communication is how it is received, regardless of the sender's intention.

Control the conversation by asking questions

As the parent of a six-year-old, I'm on a continual learning curve that reinforces how stupid I was a month ago. In parenting, your choice of language makes a difference to the outcomes you achieve. Contrast these three statements, all directed towards changing behaviour:

1 Learn your multiplication tables or you will receive a bad grade from your teacher.

2 Don't you want to be like all your friends at school and be able to recite the multiplication tables?

3 If you learn the multiplication tables, you will be able to calculate how many days we have left until Christmas.

The language you use will determine how people will respond to you. Your choice of language can influence any conversation towards being more positive, thereby gaining you greater permission to convey your message. Gaining permission for your message to be heard will influence the relationship you have with that person. The relationships you have with people — prospective clients, employees, centres of influence, colleagues and allies, existing clients — will influence your business results. It all starts with your choice of language.

You have no doubt heard the oft-quoted adage: 'There's no such thing as a stupid question.' You're kidding me! There are heaps and I hear them all the time — from salespeople, accountants, bankers, financial advisers, recruiters, lawyers and practically anyone who is responsible for marketing and business development, veteran and neophyte alike. Here are some examples of the worst:

- Who are you currently using? *None of your business.*

- Could you tell me a little about your business? *Why? Haven't you bothered to do your own research on me to discover if you can really help me?*

- Are you satisfied with your current accountant (replace this profession with any other)? *Even if I wasn't, I'm not about to admit to you that perhaps I've made lousy choice.*

- How much are you currently paying for financial planning advice? *None of your business. Just give me your best price.*

- If I could save you money, would you do business with me? *This is a very negative question and now you've educated me to make a choice simply based on price.*

- Can I send you a quote? *You can, but why bother? The next person will provide a cheaper quote to win the business, and once again you've incorrectly educated your prospective client.*

- What will it take to win your business? *What an egregious question. It's rude, lazy and disrespectful. This question doesn't even belong in used car yards anymore.*

If you are using any of these, stop it, immediately!

Whenever you are speaking you're not listening, and if you're not listening you cannot possibly learn how and why you can be of most benefit to a prospective client. If you want to wield more influence in any business conversation, you need to do the following:

- Understand the *expectations* of your clients.

- Build a positive atmosphere where everyone feels comfortable and safe enough to speak their mind candidly, to say honestly what they think. If you create this positive, relaxed atmosphere, clients are likely to provide you with more in-depth information regarding what they want.

- Pay attention to people. Listen and hear what they say. Don't assume that you know; if there is any hesitancy, ask clarification questions to ensure you have understood what the client genuinely means.

- Be persistent. Keep asking probing, intelligent, provocative questions that uncover the information you require.

- When speaking, fuel your message with client benefits and begin your discussions with agreements. When asking questions of your client always given reasons for your requests. This will help make your message understood by the client, capturing their attention and ensuring they actively listen to you.

Break mental barriers and get the client thinking your way

You cannot *not* communicate. Whenever interpersonal contact is made, communication occurs. The meanings of communication are in people, not in words. Interestingly, research has shown that while all communications are received, 70 to 90 per cent are filtered, modified or changed by the receiver. Listening is affected by selective attention, selective interpretation and selective retention. Unfortunately, as the sender you have no control over what the listener does to your communications. Let's also be clear that the function of listening is to *understand* what the other person is saying, but not necessarily to *agree* with it.

> *I know you believe you understand what you think I said, but I'm not sure you realise that what you heard is not what I meant.*
> **—Robert McCloskey**

When people get angry they tend to yell. But yelling doesn't always work. Why? Because with increased volume the words just become noise. When an email is typed in all caps for emphasis or urgency, the reader will ignore the gimmick and determine for himself or herself whether it's urgent. Pop-up website windows interrupt but are not read; instead, they're dismissed as an annoyance and reduce the likelihood of further interaction by the website visitor. When a child is yelled at by a frustrated parent, the child ignores the rants while the parent becomes even more frustrated. Yelling can easily be ignored and is a wasted effort, regardless of how urgent the message. Whispering, however, can attract attention. Paradoxically,

159

whispering can demand we take notice, because it excites our curiosity. Review how you're currently marketing: are you yelling at your customers or whispering enticingly?

Whirlpool Wisdom

- Articulate your value proposition in the form of a business outcome.

- Show your clients the return on investment in having you on board.

- Continue to market. It's not your client's job to remember you; it is your obligation to ensure they don't forget you.

How you communicate in the public domain has significant influence over the effectiveness of all your other marketing activities. What I'm suggesting is that if your marketing clearly states that you are a premium service provider, you focus on quality outcomes and you charge appropriately for that level of expertise, yet you consistently discount your fees and accommodate write-downs, you create confusion by sending two very different signals. A high degree of consistency is normally associated with personal and intellectual strength. Being consistent is sometimes stronger than being right.

1 **Change your frame of mind.** As an example, lawyers once believed it unethical to advertise and resisted most promotion and marketing activities other than networking. Now it's almost impossible to get through a television program and not be exposed to the advertising of a law firm.

2 **Appreciate that you are in the marketing business.** The technicality of your profession is the instrument you use to create a service offering that can be bought. But no longer can you simply hang up a shingle and have clients walking through the door to give you their business. Nothing happens until you have a client, and you will acquire clients only through marketing.

3 **Build a Referral Whirlpool.** Gaining referrals should be developed into a pragmatic system, with everyone in your practice educated in the process of how to ask for and acquire referrals. The best piece of advice I can give you is, don't make it hard for people to give you referrals. Do your homework and ask to be referred to a specific person. Know who you want to be referred to. Asking the blanket question, 'Who do you know who could use my services?' is lazy and does not deserve a positive response. With the best of intentions, your clients will not be able to help you because your question is too broad. By narrowing your frame of reference, you make it simpler for the client to help you. Be alert and listen for the cues that inform you that your client knows you would like to meet. And at the appropriate time, ask for a referral to that person.

4 **Aim for specificity before generalisation.** I am not recommending that you specialise and not be a generalist. I am recommending that you be known for something specific before you attempt to be known for everything. Become the go-to person for a specific reason and create a fiefdom. This does not mean that you have to knock back any business opportunity outside of the specialisation. But it does allow for people to talk about and recommend you with greater ease. If your clients don't know how to explain exactly what you do, it's difficult for them to refer you.

Understand the psychology of influence and why it's important

Social Style, a concept initially formulated by David Merrill, is perhaps the most useful model for helping people at work to understand themselves and others. Carl Jung saw a manageable way of dealing with human differences. A student of Sigmund Freud's, Jung focused much of his life's work on psychological types, archetypes, the collective unconscious, individuation and synchronicity. In *Psychological Types*, published in 1921, he describes four types of people: thinkers, fielders, intruders and sensors. These four types are premised on four questions:

- How do I take in information from the world around me?

- How do I make judgements and decisions?

- From where do I get energy?

- How much order do I prefer in my external world?

A problem with Jung's model is that as a psychological model it was about the individual's inner rather than outer behaviours, making it difficult to identify another person's style. The Myers-Briggs model, based on Jung's work, suffers from the same deficit. The psychological realities are that people operate in their own self-interest and make changes primarily based on emotion, not logic. This psychological fact is the reason why, as you will have read many times in this book, you must focus on the outcomes and not the inputs. People are primarily influenced by what they get out of something. Another psychological perspective is that people are influenced to behave by their own perceptions of:

- pride

- pleasure

- profit

- painlessness.

We all like and want to take pride in our lives. Before you give me examples to the contrary, consider the truth that although some people do not hold the same values as you, that does not mean they have less pride. While I have no inclination to ever look like 'Swampy' or dress like a Goth, I appreciate the effort of those who do take pride in their Gothic appearance and strive to be the best-looking 'Swampy' they can be. Also, please understand that profit, in this context, does not solely reference money. The profit we may be seeking could include, for example, time, stress reduction, recognition or emotional reward.

Behavioural science researchers have discovered that 75 per cent of the population is significantly different from you. We think, decide and use time differently; we work at a different pace; have varying communication styles; cope with our emotions and manage stress differently. None of this makes any one of us necessarily worse or better than any other, simply different. Behaviourally speaking, you are in the minority—as every individual is. No wonder we have people problems in the workplace, and finding a one-size-fits-all piece of marketing magic is impossible.

We will use the actions of others to delimit proper behaviour for ourselves, especially when we view those others as similar to ourselves. This 'social proof' principle, explains Robert Cialdini, author of *Influence: Science and Practice*, is used by marketers to make their messages more persuasive. So how can you use the social proof appeal in your firm's sales and marketing activities?

- Quote statistics that communicate the popularity of your service. Xero Accounting Software, for example, touts its 200 000 customers on its homepage.

- Use testimonials, case studies and success stories from satisfied clients in your presentations to prospective clients, on your website and in your sales collateral. The more similar the person giving the testimonial is to the prospect, the more persuasive the message becomes. This is why Dove doesn't use supermodels in their advertising, tip jars are always half full and buskers' collection trays are never empty.

- When you run a seminar or other event for potential clients, invite your best clients to attend. Intermingling happy clients with prospective clients increases your successful take-up of new business. When your prospects listen to your existing clients on the benefits they've received from working directly with you, they feel comfortable with accepting your approaches.

Each of these persuasive tactics builds on our natural inclination to be influenced by the behaviour of others. When a lot of people are doing something, it must be the right thing to do.

From the Front Lines

'Our feedback forms were really just a formality. Something we did because we always had. The standard form was recycled from the previous seminar with few amendments. The feedback forms were not providing any valuable information; we weren't getting a suitable return on investment from the seminars, and we certainly weren't getting any leads for new business. We reviewed the feedback form, discarded it, and wrote a completely new one. The result was outstanding! Five new leads from its first use. The question that had the greatest impact was: "Would you like us to contact you and arrange an appointment?" Basic, but forthright. Just proves that if you don't ask, you will not receive. Lesson learned: you can't keep doing the same thing and expect different results. Good enough isn't enough if you want better than ordinary results.'

—Leanne Rudd, CEO, The Money Edge

Build support and momentum for your work among others

Your existing customers, especially those who are your raving advocates, are the most powerful salespeople in your organisation. It would therefore seem axiomatic that you should have your existing customers join you on your sales calls with new prospective customers, wouldn't you think? They would be so much better than you at persuading prospective customers to buy your services and engage you. So how might you get them to join you? Have them write a testimonial for you in their own words, testifying to the value you provide and the results you've delivered. This shows what a fabulous return on investment you are, and it's much better having a customer toot your horn than doing it yourself to people who don't know you well.

Advertisers willingly spend millions of dollars for 30-second television spots during significant events such as the Olympics, the Super Bowl, grand finals or the Commonwealth Games.

That's because millions of people watch these events, so the advertisers can place their offerings in front of millions of prospective buyers. Most professional practices cannot engage in this type of expensive advertising. Instead, build your Whirlpool Marketing System: stop calling first and knocking on doors. Rather, do what's needed to position your value in front of your potential buyers, in many different ways, and continually build the momentum that will cause people to gravitate towards you and knock on your door.

Define your organisation's principles, ethics and values

Define the culture of your business as a living organism so it declares loudly who you are and what you represent. Your organisational culture provides a framework for how people will behave under pressure. It's easy to adhere to corporate policy when the waters are calm and there is wind in your sails. The real culture of your organisation bubbles to the surface during rough seas and turbulence. Ask yourself and members of your team:

- What is the core culture of our practice?
- What are the principles we hold sacrosanct and would never forfeit under any circumstances?
- What is it about our people and service offerings that create advocates for our practice?
- What will we never do?
- What are we willing to fight for?

Table 8.1 (overleaf) is an example of scheduling and tracking your marketing activities. Aim to keep the activities interesting, varied and disparate while also supporting the strategy you've created as the foundation to support the business growth objectives of your practice.

Table 8.1: Whirlpool Marketing action list

Whirlpool action	Week 1	Week 2	Week 3	Week 4	Level
Press release sent	/1				Competitive
Networking event		/1		/1	Competitive
Blog posts	/2	/2	/2	/2	Competitive
Magazine article floated			/1		Competitive
Handwritten notes sent	/5	/5	/5	/5	Distinct
Referrals requested	/3	/3	/3	/3	Distinct
Contact an association				/1	Distinct
Survey/case study, etc.				/1	Distinct
Speaking opportunity		/1			Distinct
Seminar/breakfast/event				/1	Dominant
Coffee with a Nexus	/1		/1		Dominant
Joint promotion with alliance partner		/1			Dominant
Media interview request			/1		Dominant

You Can't Make This Up

When everyone knows customer service is more critical than ever, this just shouldn't keep happening:

- I hear the words, 'This call may be recorded for training purposes', but the service continues to be lousy.

- I call a 'Help Line', which is a misnomer right from the get-go; after an interminable period of frustrating discussion, my problem remains unsolved. I give up in exasperation, only to hear those insufferable words: 'Is there anything else I can help you with today?'

- The luxury hotels I stay at charge $29.95 or thereabouts per day for internet access. This is appallingly poor judgement.

At \$600 per night, they should just increase the room rate by \$30, which no one would notice.

- When I explain to someone that I only have a minute, they acknowledge this and then ramble on ad nauseam. Did they think I was kidding?

- Why is it that the local post office cannot change a \$100 note, but the local coffee shop can?

- Oil companies should be legally banned from calling their outlets *service stations* when the person at the counter can't even swipe your credit card through the EFTPOS terminal for you. Tell me again where the service is that we receive at petrol stations?

Customer-centric culture

Ric's Tip

A positive outlook and professional pride influence your customer service success.

The physician must be able to tell the antecedents, know the present, and foretell the future—must mediate these things, and have two special objects in view with regard to disease, namely, to do good *or* to do no harm...
—Hippocratic Corpus

As professional and personal services advisers this is not enough. An accountant I know had joined a 'coaching club' of a high-profile Brisbane-based coaching firm that enlists telemarketers, uses high-pressure sales techniques and does some high-end public relations. The membership fee to join the coaching club is high. The firm, and the people running the coaching club, did nothing wrong; they just didn't do enough right. It is a 'sales machine', continually pushing members to spend more money on additional services without really delivering much improvement for the client in the interim (the accountant's words, not mine). As you deliver your professional services and expertise to your clients ask yourself three questions:

1   What is in the best interests of the client (client-organisation)?

2   How will the client (client-organisation) be better off because of your intervention?

3   If this was your company would you be willing to bet your house on the advice?

...The art consists in three things — the disease, the patient, and the physician. The physician is the servant of the art, and the patient must combat the disease along with the physician.
—Hippocratic Corpus *(cont'd)*

Engage your clients in the solution and transfer (as much as possible) the skills across to the client to produce long-lived success, even after you've gone. It's not enough to do no harm. You must do great good.

From the Front Lines

'At a Chamber of Commerce event hosted at a local restaurant, we were networking while sampling specialty dishes showcasing the chef's exquisite skills. The restaurant is known for its hot and spicy menu, and I was a little cautious. However, the staff went out of their way to provide samples from the menu that suited my tastes. I mentioned that my wife (who wasn't present) had even more difficulty with spicy foods than I did. The restaurant owner went to the kitchen, and prepared a special tasting plate to take home for my wife. She sampled the food and loved it. The next day we received a phone call from the restaurant owner asking how my wife liked the food. I often talk to my clients about giving that extra 1 per cent—this is a perfect example. Not only was it excellent customer service—it was also excellence in marketing—where the restaurant owner engaged with me, and also with my wife who wasn't present. It was achieved with a minimum of cost and effort, but a maximum amount of initiative. I regularly tell this story to my clients as an example, and my wife and I have become regular patrons at this restaurant.'

—Lester Lewis, Lester Lewis Consulting

Just because you cannot afford the marketing budget of the likes of Coca-Cola, Pepsi, Apple or McDonald's, it does not mean you shouldn't be marketing your business. It's your responsibility to share and promote the value you have to offer to those people and organisations that need what you can provide. Creating a customer-centric culture is an exceptional marketing method. Keep marketing!

How does your firm attract clients? How does your firm influence clients to circulate and interact with your organisation? Ask the right questions to develop a customer-centric perspective (see figure 8.1).

Figure 8.1: customer centricity

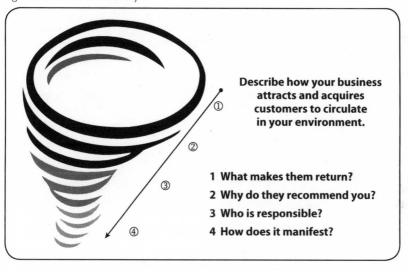

Describe how your business attracts and acquires customers to circulate in your environment.

① ② ③ ④

1 What makes them return?
2 Why do they recommend you?
3 Who is responsible?
4 How does it manifest?

Best Practices

Hotel personnel who have been asked to be more patient and courteous with guests in order to qualify for a 'most courteous employee' award can overwhelm a weary traveller without really caring about the guest at all. It's easy to focus on activity; after all it's simple to monitor and short term in nature. But it's more difficult to focus on results, which are often long term and more subjective.

Never be so arrogant as to assume what your clients should and should not buy from you. Offer multiple opportunities and allow them to make their own decisions of what value of yours they wish to access (see figure 8.2).

Figure 8.2: multiple opportunities for clients to buy

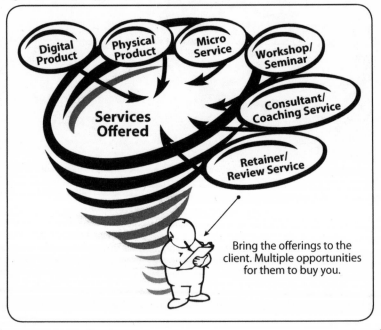

Bring the offerings to the client. Multiple opportunities for them to buy you.

Ric's Tip

New business isn't something you hunt, it's what happens while you're immersed in serving your customer. Selling without selling is the future of selling.

Your ambition is the path to your success, and it's your discipline that will drive you there. By enhancing the customer experience and making your business processes much more efficient, you cannot help but make more money through the attraction and acquisition of new business. In the new economy professional services firms need to accept that expertise alone will not grow a successful practice. It takes only seconds to destroy a person's confidence. Poor marketing decisions are guaranteed to destroy the confidence of even the best experts and leaders. 'It's not personal, just business.' Easy advice to give, but not so easy to accept. Most of us are not insensitive and our feelings do matter, even if we try not to show it. A customer berates you and your organisation for what they perceive as lousy service. The product you're selling keeps getting returned by purchasers who say it doesn't fulfil the promises made. The colleague you used to play a round of golf with each month now never seems to have the time.

How well do you know your customers? Honestly, you don't know them intimately, any more than they know you intimately. How well do you know your staff? You don't know everything about them and they certainly don't know everything about you. But they do know themselves and you know yourself. When a client chooses a new accountant, it's not about you; it's a personal choice they make for themselves. When a colleague now prioritises their time so that golf has dropped to the bottom of their list, they've made a personal decision; it's not about denying you. Do your work and live your life the best way you can ... for you. It's personal for you, it's not about anyone else.

Professional Services Marketing Wisdom

If a buyer rejects your proposal, if a colleague or peer disagrees with your analysis, if an editor rejects your article submission, get over it. Being rejected is not an indictment of you. So what if you get rejected this time? It's their prerogative to say no, and it's yours to have a different opinion and to continue trying.

The productivity paradox

The best way to create powerful customer relationships is to respond in real time. A personal meeting has significantly more impact than a letter. A telephone conversation gives greater connection than an email. When you work to another person's schedule your productivity nosedives. Because you're responding to their urgency and not your priorities, your time management is history and your routine destroyed. Decisions have to be made by you; prioritise the importance of your customer interactions. Schedule blocks of time to do the important, serious, uninterrupted work and be comfortable knowing that you've made a decision that is in the best interest of your future success. After all, you need to continue to be successful to remain in business, to provide ongoing service to your customers. Schedule blocks of time when you can respond to customers in real time by picking up the telephone or meeting for coffee.

Balance is vital. Getting the two priorities aligned to ensure your own productivity while developing real-time relationships is your key to great business results.

172

CHAPTER 9

Rules for results in relationships and proposals

Marketing goes wrong when it is perceived as a bolt-on activity.
Michael Perry

A common mistake in marketing and selling professional services is failing to build the proper peer-level relationship and using the proposal as an exploration of *whether* you will be doing business together, rather than a summation of *how* you will be working together given the level of agreement previously reached around the objectives. The proposal is the easy part, if all the other business relationship building blocks are based on a strong foundation. Speed bumps can still be just around the bend, so to ensure a smooth journey, engage the prospective client to help you write the proposal. This guarantees there are no surprises for the client and they are in agreement with the premise of your submission. And, as the co-creator of the proposal, the client is far more inclined to buy into the project.

In this chapter you learn how to:

* improve your success before you send a proposal

* develop agreement before writing your proposal

* never be perceived as a 'used car salesman'

* suggest options that are valuable for your client and provide more revenues for you.

Much of this book is dedicated to explaining what we can do to create success. There is relevance in also considering what not to do. There is nothing new under the sun, and mistakes in marketing of professional services are commonplace. Many mistakes should never happen, and perhaps their recurrence is due primarily to ignorance or forgetfulness. Here are some of them:

- **Failing to speak directly to your prospective clients.** Your prospective clients and existing clients have problems, wants and needs for which you have the solutions. Your marketing should speak directly to your clients, illuminating the issues and showing how you are the solution. Your language must be concise, your message conveying with clarity specifically what you can do for them and what benefits they will gain by engaging your services. You've missed the point if your marketing is focused on you, your methodologies and your fees.

- **Failing to seek feedback from your existing clients.** Two-way communication invites feedback and input that educates you on how to be of even better service to your existing clientele. For instance, through client feedback you can be made aware of other issues and challenges your clients currently face or are likely to face. With this knowledge you can anticipate customer needs, develop new products and services, and form new partnerships and/or alliances that provide the solutions that your clients will buy.

- **Promoting features instead of benefits.** Clients do not buy services, they buy solutions. Just as they don't buy your time, they buy your expertise. Your marketing should inform and educate clients about what you can do for them and the benefits they will receive from engaging you and receiving your professional advice.

- **Sending mixed messages.** You cannot over-communicate when you're delivering value. However, too many mixed messages will only create confusion. A marketing brochure or advertising is not a shopping list of goodies you've got for sale. There is no need to put everything in a brochure or an advertisement. Focus on two or three key points and then direct the reader to where they can access more information, such as your website.

- **Marketing in the wrong media.** Copying what your competitors do to be successful does not guarantee you the same results. You must determine what the most appropriate media are for you to reach your audience. Where do your clients go for the information they are looking for? What do they read? What organisations do they belong to? Where do they network? That's where your marketing should be positioned.

- **Having unprofessional marketing materials.** Your marketing collateral is a direct reflection of you and your professionalism. Photocopied brochures are amateurish and should be left to the neophytes. In this new world of digital printing, you can easily and cost-effectively design and produce high-quality marketing materials ranging from business cards to brochures to booklets. But unless your profession is in graphic design, outsource this to an expert who does it for a living. You have more important things to do with your time.

- **Offering non-differentiated services.** In their book *Funky Business*, authors Jonas Ridderstrale and Kjell Nordström refer to the proliferation of business clichés as the 'surplus society': 'A surplus of similar companies, employing similar people, with similar educational backgrounds, coming up with similar ideas, producing similar things, with similar prices and similar quality.' If your offerings are the same as your competitors', then your only point of leverage to win the business is price. There is no such thing as a commodity practice, only practices that are marketed like commodities. The key to growing any professional services firm is having the ability to differentiate your service offerings from those of your competitors. By offering differentiated services you have the freedom to charge the fees you are worth and have your clients gladly pay you, and to develop additional revenue streams outside your mainstream business.

- **Assuming your market understands what you offer.**
  Your potential customers are unlikely to understand or
  appreciate the intricacies of your expertise and capabilities.
  By providing a more direct and clear explanation of the
  services you offer, the solutions you provide and the
  improvements these will deliver, you will more likely
  influence the client to choose you.

- **Failing to offer options.** When you provide a prospective
  client with a single solution, you have immediately limited
  your ability to convert the prospect into a client. A single
  take-it-or-leave-it option is akin to playing roulette and only
  betting on black. At best, you have a 50–50 chance — not
  good odds. Alternatively, by providing a prospective client
  with three options of varying value, you've immediately
  improved the odds in your favour. The client is no longer
  choosing whether or not to do business with you, but instead,
  which of your three options makes the most sense for them.

- **Positioning your business incorrectly.** How you position
  your business will have a direct impact on the types of
  customers you will attract. You know why your business is
  different. You're clear about what types of clients are ideal
  for your practice. You understand how you're better than
  the competition. It's imperative that you communicate these
  points to the right people, through the right media, in the
  most appropriate fashion.

- **Ignoring the visceral connection.** This is especially true
  for accountants, lawyers, bankers, and other professionals
  educated in a financial discipline or according to a rational
  doctrine. Logic allows us to think rationally, but we make
  buying decisions based on emotion. Your marketing messages
  should appeal to both aspects.

- **Not collecting client information.** Your database of
  customers is one of the strategic assets of your business.
  Your clients often belong to and draw on a rich tapestry of
  networks and communities, a resource that could keep you
  happily productive for a lifetime.

- **Not understanding why customers leave.** Very few professional practices make a personalised effort to understand why a customer has taken their business elsewhere. Completing an exit interview with lost clients will identify problems in your practice of which you are unaware. Those problems can then be corrected. An exit interview will identify what alternative services are being offered by competitors that enable them to attract your clientele away. It is recommended that you engage an external resource to complete the exit interviews, as the client may be less hesitant to provide them with candid and honest responses.

- **Not asking for referrals.** Despite their generally acknowledged benefits, very few professional practices have implemented a formal referral system. And very few practices engage in professional education to learn how to successfully ask for and receive quality referrals. Many professionals are reluctant even to ask for referrals, in spite of the fact that they gladly give them.

- **Failing to implement a Marketing Whirlpool.** Marketing is both art and science, and should be one of the constants of your daily business activity. Diverse, disparate and fun marketing activities should account for 40 minutes of your daily business regime. Business owners—not just professional practitioners—make three common mistakes with marketing:

  1 They reduce marketing investment during soft or difficult economic times.

  2 They ignore marketing activities during busy periods.

  3 They fail to invest in marketing during positive economic times when business is good.

These mistakes are tactical in nature. A strategic mistake is to focus only on attracting new customers rather than on retaining and developing existing customers. You're in the relationship business, and most marketing activities best suited to professionals rely on healthy client relationships. Your clients are exposed to more choice than ever before, and if you fail to care for them as they expect, someone else will. The best way to do this is to create true value that benefits them and achieves their goals. You can no longer take your clients for granted; if you haven't already, you must quickly develop a passion for nurturing and understanding your clients and their unique needs. You know how you like to be treated as a customer — that's how you must treat yours. While most professional practices will have a *commitment to customer service* written somewhere in their Procedures and Operations Manual, you can achieve a fundamental business advantage by embracing a culture of *commitment to your customers*.

You Can't Make This Up

Landing late at Melbourne airport due to flight delays, I hurry out with John, my regular limo driver, to drive to my first meeting, for which I'm already five minutes late. A crookedly parked vehicle alongside necessitates that I sit in the front passenger seat rather than the rear. John wastes no time and in moments we're racing along the freeway into the CBD at speeds that risk attracting official attention.

The iPhone rings and I quickly answer. The caller wishes to speak with Yusef. 'You have the wrong number.' The caller apologises and hangs up. Moments later it rings again. The caller asks to speak with Yusef. 'You have the wrong number. There is no Yusef here and I've had the number since 1989.' At this point, my long-time driver looks at me, looks at the phone and chuckles. 'Mr Ric, *my* name is Yusef, and that's not *your* iPhone.'

Business relationships strengthen and bond not only through what is true and successful, but also through the errors and failings.

David Smith is the Managing Director of DAME Consulting, a technology commercialisation and commercial negotiation company providing consulting services to the global energy and resources industry. Smith's previous leadership roles with GHD and Linc Energy contribute to his expert opinions on how to be a successful marketer of high-value professional services. The key attributes demanded of any professional who wishes to work for him include: intelligence, a thirst for new knowledge, assertiveness, self-motivation and a good memory. A successful international negotiator, Smith counsels that as a professional you must be bold while maintaining a humble demeanour. He attributes his own personal success in the engineering and energy sectors to a number of specific marketing activities and business development philosophies. These are relevant for almost all kinds of professional services.

- Have boardroom lunches and coffees. Inviting clients and prospects to your boardroom to share information, network and learn about new developments are powerful positioning opportunities. Smith declares that many times he never had to ask for the business—opportunities were offered by clients at these boardroom meetings.

- Join the boards of associations. It's not enough to be a member; you have to get on the leadership committee or board so everyone knows who you are, even if you have to nominate yourself for the position.

- Meet clients in social settings. It will help the client reveal worthwhile information about what they want and need from you and your services.

- Use appropriate communication. How you interact and communicate depends on who you're engaged with at the time. How you communicate with a CEO may be different from how you communicate with an engineer or a government employee.

- Be a good listener. Know when to shut up and stop trying to sell or promote yourself. It's not necessary to be dominant in negotiations. Put your ego aside.

- Develop a compelling story that appeals to the client's needs and gives them a solution that makes you their obvious choice.

Smith emphasises the importance of a willingness to work outside normal business hours. 'You have to go to and be seen at everything. Go out of your way to network wherever your potential will be.'

He advises professionals responsible for business development to conscientiously:

- build a contact list and continually connect with those people
- ask for referrals and give referrals regularly
- be consistent so clients are comfortable with you
- cultivate positive word-of-mouth recommendations.

Smith warns, 'You have to understand that sometimes there are bonds that clients have with your competition that cannot be broken, and you will never win that business.'

His final piece of advice for leaders: 'The last person you dismiss from your employ is your marketer.'

What you must do to improve your success before you send a proposal

A prevalent mistake is not appreciating the importance of building peer-level relationships, and instead acting as a vendor. An example of this is using the proposal as an exploration of *whether* you will be doing business together, rather than as a summation of *how* you will be doing business together, given the level of agreement previously reached around the objectives for the client. The proposal is the easy part, if all the other building blocks have been stacked correctly. Of course there may be speed bumps just around the bend. To ensure the journey is smooth, engage the prospective client to help you write the proposal. This guarantees that there are no surprises for the client, and that they are in agreement with the premise of your submission. Furthermore the client, as the co-creator of the proposal, is far more inclined to accept and buy into the project.

The headache for many lies in the invitation, 'Send me a proposal'. The truth is most proposals should never be written. The proposal does not win the business for you. Most are written as explorations, seeking to discover some (any) interest from the prospective client. The proposal will rarely be the deciding factor on whether the customer will choose to do business with you. If you have not discussed how you might do business with the prospective client, if you have not reached agreement on what is to be achieved, if you have not established the client's genuine needs, then the proposal will not win business.

My observations of accountants, business coaches, consultants, financial planners, recruiters, trainers and the like indicate that they mistakenly believe that a proposal can convert tyre-kickers and window–shoppers into serious buyers.

Manage your mindset and understand that the proposal should be a summary of agreement. Rather than exploring the possibilities through the lengthy and time-consuming process of writing a proposal, it's far more expedient to sit down with the client and ask intelligent questions to assess your value to them. When the next prospective customer ominously invites you to 'send me a proposal', pause, relax and calmly respond, 'I'd be delighted. But so I don't waste your time, there are some things I need to hear from you personally. Let's arrange for coffee on Tuesday and share 20 minutes. I can ask you a few questions and guarantee that my proposal will be useful for both of us.'

Best Practices

Bite your tongue: When a prospective client asks what you can do for them, stop yourself from reciting a shopping list of available options, or from giving them the hour-long sermon on your favourite solution. Ask questions to determine what the client needs rather than what you want to give them.

Develop agreement before writing a proposal

Prior to writing and sending your proposal, reach agreement with your client on what the proposal will contain. By making the effort to reach agreement in advance of writing the proposal you save an enormous amount of time. The objective is to identify how your services will improve the customer's condition and to establish clear outcomes considering any available factors.

First of all, both parties should agree to the objectives, outcomes and goals, and the value that would be gained as a result of your involvement. Establishing objectives is the initial point of any project. To achieve conformity with the client's wants and needs, you have to look at the key factors and elicit from the client outcome-based business objectives. Review these with the client to clarify that you've understood what was discussed in the manner the client assumed. As your investigations into the client's needs and objectives continue, dive deeper to uncover the expected results.

These are some questions to guide you through the process:

- How would conditions improve because of this project?

- Ideally, what would the client like to accomplish?

- What are expectations in terms of return on investment?

- How will you be evaluated in terms of the project achievement?

- Will there be major differences brought about by the services you are offering?

- Is the client expecting something that you can't deliver?

Taking this approach helps to eliminate the possibility of scope creep and any misunderstanding about exactly what services will and won't be performed. The goals and the limits of the services to be rendered will be implicit and agreed upon. The client is maximising your input and talents on the project to make them as effective as possible for him and as rewarding as possible for you. Beginning with objectives, you then prepare a framework within which the services can be rendered.

Whirlpool Wisdom

Your proposal should provide options that allow the client to choose how, and at what level of investment, they will engage your services. It should not, however, detail the pricing of individual components of service within the project. You're a professional providing expert advice, not a restaurateur with a menu. Component pricing educates the client that you're a commodity, and they are now free to pick and choose individual components at will. If that happens, you've lost control of the relationship and you'll probably lose the business to another adviser who decides to undersell you. Your objective is for your client to evaluate your intervention and compare the return on investment, not to compare your module pricing with that of other advisers.

You need to consider how to:

- establish agreement with the client for what the proposal must contain

- avoid competitive 'pitching' for business, and why you will lose if you don't

- structure stages into your proposal and make it easy for the client to 'give it a try'.

Why you don't want to be a 'used car salesman'

You can fool some of the people all of the time, and all of the people some of the time, but you cannot fool all of the people all of the time.
—Abraham Lincoln

Crafty salespeople can convince a customer to buy a product or service that's not totally necessary. Remember under-car protection coating? Along with rust, paint fade, rock chip and interior fabric protection? And the ultimate up–sell: interior sound protection? A venue may cancel a prior sales order because a higher offer has since been made. Or a technician finds imaginary fault with machinery or equipment to get a short–lived bump in this month's sales quotas. But consumers will no longer be duped, as Sainsbury's discovered with their bogus half-price Breville sandwich maker. Poor customer service will no longer be tolerated, even a little. Long-lasting success is created by building profitable long–term relationships that lead to trust and respect. It's not as easy, but it is far more satisfying for both you and your customer. Manipulation is not professional, nor is it necessary.

Unlike selling cars, selling professional services is a transformation of agreement and a reinforcement of relationships (see figure 9.1). Unlike selling a commodity, the engagement never ends and the opportunities to do further good work are limited only by your willingness to serve.

Figure 9.1: transforming prospects into engaged clients

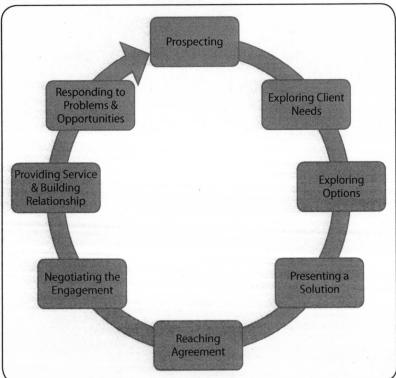

From the Front Lines

Just six weeks before the original iPhone was announced, Apple CEO Steve Jobs chose an option for the phone that was not. Jobs decided that the iPhone should have a scratch-proof glass screen. But it wasn't one of the design options. It wasn't tested and so engineers weren't sure it would be even feasible, let alone reliable. Nobody was certain that it could be done, especially within such a short time frame. Any other CEO would have not considered it an option, at least this time around, given the constraints and doubts. Organisations declare they want to be innovators, to be remarkable, to achieve excellence, but how many are willing to attempt what's unreasonable? How many are prepared to choose the option that is not?

Getting fired from Apple was the best thing that could have ever happened to me. The heaviness of being successful was replaced by the lightness of being a beginner again. It freed me to enter one of the most creative periods of my life.
— **Steve Jobs**

Suggest options that are valuable for your client and provide more revenue for you

The shorter you can make your proposals, the more likely they are to be read and accepted by your clients. Proposals longer than five pages have a greater likelihood of being referred to head office, the legal department, general counsel or external lawyers. Any or all of these people will decide it's their responsibility to find fault or adduce problems, thereby justifying their interference and delaying acceptance of your proposal.

The proposal template I'm providing you with is of a generic style that can be adapted and adopted by most professional and personal services, such as accounting and auditing, law, business consulting and coaching, financial advisory and planning, HR and recruitment, training, professional speaking, IT, counselling and mental health.

The proposal includes these components:

- *situational summary*—why professional expertise is being sought

- *objectives and goals*—the objectives, goals and outcomes being sought by the client from your intervention

- *metrics that indicate success*—the measurable indicators that will demonstrate progress towards successfully achieving the agreed-upon objectives and goals

- *value*—the value (both tangible and intangible) for the client of improvement, increased results and elimination of problems

- *methodology, transfer mechanisms and options*—itemised list of implementation choices

- *accountabilities*—client responsibilities that must be fulfilled and your own responsibilities

- *scheduling*—commencement date, duration and completion date (specific dates, not generalised periods of time)

- *terms and conditions*—fees, reimbursements and the scheduling of such

- *agreement to proceed*—instructions on how the client is to nominate their option choice and arrange for deposit payment.

To be more successful than the average, your proposals need to be a summation of the agreement between you and your client about what the objectives, goals and metrics are, and the value to the client of your professional involvement. (Bullet points always make for clearer reading than pages of narrative.) Proposals should not be a fishing expedition, nor should they be negotiating documents. The proposal should not contain excess verbiage or lists of terms and conditions, or it will end up being referred to your client's head office administrators, which will be about as much fun as having the skin peeled from your eyeballs.

Sean O'Donnell, Managing Director of Mindbank Australia, has been a banking executive responsible for leading business development personnel for over two decades. O'Donnell has acquired key client-relationship knowledge that is transferable across most professions. Here's his core advice to professionals responsible for acquiring new business:

- Have good self-esteem. Be confident in yourself, your company and your services.

- Value your time. Time is a non-renewable resource that must never be wasted.

- Create systems, templates and processes to automate your work as much as possible.

- Understand your customer, and their goals and aspirations.

- Provide an exceptional level of customer service such as they've never experienced before.

- Focus on the value that you deliver.

- Probe beyond the client's wants to uncover their needs.

- Help the client to fully understand why some options are better than others; give them choices.

- Make customer satisfaction your ultimate priority.

- Seek to influence by focusing on what's best for the client, not for you.

- Do the things your competitors cannot do, and make a difference to your client.

- Pay most attention to articulating the benefits and value to your client, and less on your fee.

O'Donnell believes that professional services providers need to tuck their egos away, to admit that they need development in soft skills, and to be willing to reach into their own pocket and pay for their education. 'What I've learned through my 25-year career as a banking executive is that the most powerful branding you can achieve is *trust*.'

CHAPTER 10

Selective acquisition: choose the keepers and release the others

Use the same measure for selling that you use for purchasing.
Abu Bakr

It's common for clients to attempt to negotiate your fees. You will be happiest and most successful if you choose the most appropriate clients for your firm, rather than accepting everyone who walks through your door. By selectively choosing who you *will* and who you *will not* take on as clients, you strengthen the value and longevity of your firm. By constantly assessing the worth of your clients to your business, you protect yourself from the vagaries of clients who may not respect you or the value you deliver.

In this chapter you learn how to:

- design your own Client Assessment Profile

- relinquish the wrong type of client, and the reasons for doing so

- build high value to justify your price

- negotiate lower fees, when appropriate, without losing credibility.

A lousy prospect never becomes a great client. Not every client is a good client; in fact, bad clients can squeeze good clients out of your organisation. A bad client is one who doesn't add value to your enterprise or bottom line, affords you no professional satisfaction and doesn't enhance your reputation. Low-value clients are unprofitable and there's simply no rational purpose in retaining this type of business. They will deplete the resources of your organisation and your people, create anxiety and frustration, and wear you down. This will take your focus away from delivering exceptional results and outcomes to your A-class clients, and they will walk. You need to respect yourself, your staff and your professionalism enough to have these bad clients exit the system.

'But at least their dollars help cover our overhead.'

Those dollars actually have a negative value to your business when you and your team become demoralised. How much does it cost you to replace a staff member who leaves? How much does it cost your reputation in the marketplace when a good client becomes disgruntled with your work? How much does it cost your family when you regularly work late to satisfy the unreasonable demands of these bad clients? Not every dollar is a good dollar. The only kind of business you should want is smart business. Income is vanity but profit is sanity.

Design your own Client Assessment Profile

A client assessment profile will provide valuable insights as to whether you should pursue a prospective client, and possibly whether you should accept them as a client. By creating the assessment profile in a spreadsheet program, you are able to answer a set of criteria and allocate a rating number for the criteria, which helps you to determine the worth of the prospective client. Any assessment profile is subjective, but if developed wisely, and further honed as you learn more about your business and where you wish to be positioned, it can be of great value. This assessment profile can and should be used by everyone in the firm to ascertain the quality of prospects and clients that your organisation pursues. Figure 10.1 provides an example of an assessment profile as a reference to assist you in creating a profile that is specific to your practice and objectives. You need to cover the individual areas of importance with regard to client engagement for your practice. You can access our Client Assessment Profile online and test it out on your existing clients by going to executivewisdom.com/wiley-psmw-cap.

Figure 10.1: the Executive Wisdom Client Assessment Profile

Executive Wisdom Client Profile Assessment

Client	Additional Business	Appeal of Engagement	Client Satisfaction	Client Source	Complexity	Payment Ease	Profitability	Referral	Risk	Score	Rating
Acme Accountants	2	3	4	1	5	4	2	3	5	29	B
Betta Bankers	3	1	5	2	4	4	2	1	4	26	C
Catalyst Coaching	4	2	3	3	5	2	2	2	5	28	B
Delta Diagnostics	4	4	4	4	2	3	5	5	2	36	A
Estate Property	3	4	3	4	2	2	4	4	2	28	B
Frugal Financial Advisers	2	1	2	4	2	4	2	1	3	18	X
Grateful Gardeners	4	4	4	4	3	5	3	4	5	36	A
Harry's Hairdressing	5	5	5	4	4	4	2	2	3	35	B
Ingot Mining	5	5	5	5	1	5	5	5	1	37	A
Jumpin' Jaques	1	2	1	2	4	1	1	1	5	18	X
Kelvin's Kitchen Kupboards	2	3	2	1	4	1	1	1	3	18	X
Leesa's Lawyers	5	5	4	5	2	5	5	5	3	39	A
Maxim Movers	3	1	3	3	3	3	1	1	5	23	C

Scoring guide

Additional Business	Appeal of Engagement	Client Satisfaction	Client Source	Complexity	Payment Ease	Profitability	Referral	Risk
5 : Significant potential	5 : Client / project is very appealing to our business & our people	5 : Client is enthusiastic about our offering, service & people	5 : Tied to an existing A category client	5 : Little to no complexity of concern which imposes burdens	5 : Always pays within terms, without complaint	5 : Maximum profitability client	5 : Excellent advocate and regularly refers opportunities	5 : No risk
4 : Known additional potential	4 : Client / project is quite appealing to our business & our people	4 : Client is positive and grateful of our offering, service & people	4 : Referred by an A class strategic alliance, partner or peer	4 : Some complexity; but can be handled with existing internal resources	4 : Pays within terms with little question of price & value	4 : Significant profitability	4 : Advocate with intermittent referrals	4 : Below or average risk
3 : Zero currently; but future potential	3 : Client / project is good work but doesn't stimulate our business & our people	3 : Client is thankful but less than exuberant	3 : Tied to an existing B category client	3 : Some complexity which necessitates senior expertise involvement	3 : Pays within terms but regularly seeks discounts or other latitude	3 : Above average profitability	3 : Good word-of-mouth and refers if asked	3 : Some risk
2 : Zero currently; future doubtful	2 : Client / project can be fulfilled but would prefer other business	2 : Client was at times unrealistic, demanding and not forthcoming	2 : Tied to another client, alliance or peer	2 : Complex requiring additional resources, expertise & high level involvement	2 : Pays outside of terms and frequently seeks discounts & complains	2 : Average profitability	2 : Refers only if asked and lacks enthusiasm	2 : Above average risk
1 : Does not value our offerings	1 : Only engaging client / project for lack of other opportunity	1 : Client hates us and treated our people poorly	1 : No significant referral or ties	1 : Very complex requiring external resources adding costs	1 : Never pays within terms, seeks discounts and complains	1 : Less than average profitability	1 : Provides no negative appraisal but no positive either	1 : High risk

In the Executive Wisdom Client Assessment Profile you can apply the scoring system outlined in table 10.1. You will of course need to assess your clients and potential clients using criteria that make sense for you and your business, rather than adopting this assessment exactly as presented here.

Table 10.1: additional business

Additional business	
Points	**Assessment**
5	There is significant potential to do additional work with this client.
4	There is some potential for additional work with this client.
3	There is no additional business currently, but there is future potential.
2	There is no additional business currently, and future additional work is doubtful.
1	The client does not value your offerings.
Appeal of the engagement	
Points	**Assessment**
5	The client or project is very appealing to your business and your people.
4	The client or project is of above-average appeal to your business and your people.
3	The client or project is good work but doesn't stimulate you, your business or your people.
2	The project can be fulfilled but you would prefer other (a different type of) business.
1	You're only engaging the client or project for lack of other income-generating opportunities.
Client satisfaction	
Points	**Assessment**
5	The client is enthusiastic about your offering, service and people.
4	The client is positive and grateful of your offering, service and people.
3	The client is thankful but less than exuberant.
2	The client was/is at times unrealistic, demanding and not forthcoming.
1	The client dislikes you and treated your people poorly.

Client source	
Points	*Assessment*
5	The client is tied to an existing A-class client.
4	The client was referred by an A-class strategic alliance, partner or peer.
3	The client is tied to an existing B-category client.
2	The client is tied to another client, alliance or peer.
I	There are no significant referrals or ties.
Complexity	
Points	*Assessment*
5	The work has little to no complexity that imposes burdens on your firm.
4	There is some complexity, but it can be handled with existing internal resources.
3	There is some complexity that necessitates senior expertise involvement.
2	The complexity requires additional resources, expertise and high-level involvement.
I	The work is very complex, requiring external resources that add costs.
Payment ease	
Points	*Assessment*
5	The client always pays within your standard terms, without complaint.
4	The client always pays within your standard terms, with little question of price and value.
3	The client always pays within your standard terms, but regularly seeks discounts or other latitude.
2	The client pays outside of your standard terms, and frequently seeks latitude.
I	The client never pays within your standard terms, and often seeks discounts or complains.

(continued)

Table 10.1: additional business *(cont'd)*

Profitability	
Points	**Assessment**
5	This is a maximum profitability client.
4	This is a significant profitability client.
3	This is an above-average profitability client.
2	This is an average profitability client.
1	This is a less than average profitability client.
Referral	
Points	**Assessment**
5	The client is an excellent advocate and regularly refers opportunities.
4	The client is an advocate with intermittent referrals offered.
3	The client provides good word-of-mouth and refers if asked.
2	The client refers only if asked and lacks enthusiasm.
1	The client provides no positive or negative appraisal.
Risk	
Points	**Assessment**
5	The client and their work present no risk.
4	The client and their work present below-average or average risk.
3	The client and their work present some risk.
2	The client and their work present above-average risk.
1	The client and their work present high risk.

It is vital you answer candidly for each client and criterion. Client value is established and determined on much more than revenues and profits. The Executive Wisdom Client Profile Assessment assists you in ascertaining and clarifying the best and the worst clients within your organisation. While some are great for your organisation, others actually cost you more than they bring in. No doubt you have experienced them before—those who are quick to complain, slow to pay, and push the boundaries by demanding more than was agreed to.

The Executive Wisdom Client Profile Assessment helps you:

1   focus on the better clients of your organisation

2   quantify the better clients of your organisation

3   identify the (A-class) clients you must focus more of your attention on

4   ascertain the (B-class) clients having the potential of rating higher on the diagnostic

5   recognise those (C-class) clients who need to be managed up or managed out in a reasonable time frame

6   determine the X-class clients and carefully consider how you will release them.

From the Front Lines

'When the global financial crisis hit I wasn't being asked to write as many financial plans. I realised governments had large numbers of staff who would still receive substantive superannuation payments at retirement. Nonetheless, those who were two or three years from retirement were worried about how they would make ends meet once they stopped working. I created a 40-minute information seminar focused only on schoolteachers with less than five years until retirement. The seminar was free and at the conclusion of each, I offered a one-hour consultation with a summary assessment of their circumstances. For $500 each I was selling peace of mind and a financial planning appointment two or three years in advance. I was averaging six or more per week and I had a book of appointments to write full financial plans over the ensuing years.'

—Trevor Feldman, CFP

Ric's Tip

Bad neighbours drive out the good neighbours. Pretty soon, the whole neighbourhood has changed so much that the real estate prices plunge and the quality of the neighbourhood becomes unattractive.

Relinquish the wrong type of client – and the reasons for doing so

Just because you have the ability to do something, it does not mean it's your responsibility to do it. A subordinate asks you to do something for them because they tell you they're unable to do it. This is called dumping the wet baby. Yes, you have the ability to do what your subordinate needs done. But should you? No. It's not your responsibility. It's the subordinate's responsibility and they need to learn how to do it for themselves.

'You know what? It's quicker if I just do it myself.' You're right … the first time, and possibly the second time. But the third time and onwards this is not the case. Taking the time now, today, to educate that person will require more time invested by you … this time. You may have to recap the training a second time also. Will this take you longer than doing it yourself? Probably. But now this person does know how to do it and will no longer require your input or oversight. You will recoup your time investment in educating that person, which will begin to save you time.

Sometimes the best way to help someone is to *not* help them. The same philosophy can be applied to retaining those clients that are not ideal for you and your practice. Are you able to do their work? Yes. Should you do their work and keep them as a client? Perhaps not.

As I travel the globe speaking at accounting, legal and financial planning conferences, especially, I am always asked for my opinions on how to attract professional staff. It seems that no matter what country I am in, these three professions are always searching to hire quality professionals. Although the focus of this book is marketing rather than recruitment, I suggest you consider analysing your employment issues from a different perspective for just one moment. I'm not assuming that the practices in these three professions don't need more staff. But perhaps they don't require as many as they might believe. By tweaking the business model of the practice, revenues can be increased without necessarily increasing professional staff numbers, and at the same time the current staff can achieve a more balanced work–life ratio.

If your practice is at competent capacity, rather than working longer hours (which is unhealthy and ineffective, and negatively affects the quality of work produced), it's time to let go, reach out and reach up. Let go of the bottom 15 per cent of your clients, reach out into the marketplace and market your services only to A-class clients, and reach up to deliver higher quality services at higher fee levels. Easier said than done, right? Putting it bluntly, the only reason any professional hesitates when I provide this advice is *fear of the unknown*.

You need to make the time to market, and market in a way that matters to the clients that matter to you. Every two years, consider jettisoning the bottom 10 to 15 per cent of business. The purpose is to relieve you of process activity, enabling you to complete ongoing marketing activities to attract new, quality business. If your practice is not generating the revenues or profitability that you expect, but you're too busy for marketing, then you're doing your practice, and your people, a disservice.

Determining what business you must let go of requires more thought than picking off clients based on their fee levels or your gut feeling. Run your clients through a client assessment profile diagnostic (such as the one I've provided in this chapter) and make a list of the X-class and C-class clients you currently have on your books. Bring your team together and rapidly make a final assessment (for the sake of your, your people's and your practice's health and survival) of which clients you must let go.

1   Is the client an advocate for our firm, providing excellent referrals and positive word-of-mouth?

2   Has the client grown and have we grown with the client over the past two years?

3   Does the client really need our talents, or could anyone do their work?

4   Is the fee at the level we deserve?

5   Is this client adding to our image and reputation?

6   Are we proud to cite this client as a reference to our expertise?

Remember, you have asked the six questions above of an X- or C-class client. If your team cannot unanimously respond in the affirmative to at least four of the six questions, it's time for you to graciously recommend this client to another professional (a practice that is at the stage of its life cycle where your practice was five years or so ago), who would appreciate them as a client. When I was young and single the two-door convertible sports cars I would buy every three or four years were perfect for my lifestyle and me. As a 49-year-old married father of a 6-year-old girl, those vehicles just aren't appropriate. Circumstances change and so must our choices. It's our obligation to behave responsibly towards ourselves and the people in our care.

Best Practices

'My professional practice has changed and we're no longer capable of providing you with the level of service and attention that you deserve. It would be inappropriate of me to take advantage of our relationship by continuing our professional engagement when it's not in your best interests. I can introduce you to a few fine professionals who are better placed to serve you and have expressed interest in handling your requirements. I appreciate your past business relationship with us and am grateful that we've had this time working together.'

Build high value to justify your price

In a previous life I left the employ of a chartered accounting firm to start my own tax practice in partnership with a friend. My partner was the accounting genius so I was left with business development, marketing and building client relationships. I made a conscious decision that we would not burden ourselves with time sheets. Accountants and lawyers are fascinated with this administrative function of recording six-minute time increments to be billed against a client file. In all my interactions with clients I gave them a fixed price upfront. Sometimes we won the business and sometimes we lost it, because I never low-balled our pricing. As a start-up business with zero clients, neither my partner nor I could afford to work for less.

Our approach was that we would charge what was considered an appropriate fee for our work and our expertise. If the prospective client said we were too expensive, I never reduced my price. I wished them well and realised I had not done enough to explain the value and significant return on their investment we offered. My fault, not the client's. With one less client, I now had time to market to more key prospects. If my partner and I had done work on the cheap just because we were starting out, I never would have had the time to market our services. This approach to pricing and value worked very well for us in the tax practice, and it is working well for me as an OD consultant.

Throughout this book, we have continually discussed 'value', and the implication has been that the term also reflects fees. Typically, most professionals remain slaves to hourly (or per diem) pricing and benchmarking those against their competition. Again, that is a reflection of value as perceived by the client. Standard economic theory of supply and demand is inappropriate for the purposeful pricing policy of your professional practice. Your clients care only about the improvement you make to them in their business and have little regard for how much time it requires of you. The client cannot be sure that you actually worked the number of hours you billed for. Neither can they be certain that you achieved what was possible in the time you worked. Hourly pricing is unethical and illogical.

How and when to raise your fees

Value-based fees and hourly pricing aside, the question remains: how and when do you raise your fees?

1 **You reach competent capacity.** Everyone has only
   24 hours in a day, so if you've reached competent capacity,
   your choices are to employ more resources, work longer
   hours or raise your fees. The default position is to work
   longer hours, which is unhealthy, unsustainable and inimical
   to maintaining quality. So you employ another staff member,
   which brings with it so many more issues and challenges that
   eat into any time you may have gained with the employment
   of the new person. Raise your fees.

2 **Your fees are the same as they were two years ago.**
Your business has grown, your brand is strong, your quality
is high and your fees have stagnated; it's time to raise your
fees. The fee increase can be a multi-step process if you're
uncomfortable with an across-the-board change. By staging
the increments in your fees for the different segments in your
business, the transition for your staff and your clients can be
more palatable. As an example:
  i. Fee levels are increased for all new clients.
  ii. Fee levels are increased for X- and C-class clients.
  iii. Fee levels are increased for all new projects.
  iv. Fee levels are increased for all existing clients.

3 **Your specialisation is not easily replicated.** Specialist
medical practitioners are always more expensive than
your GP. We know this, we expect it and we pay the price
without equivocation. We believe the specialist has unique
knowledge and skills that can help us where our GP cannot.
If your practice or individuals within your practice have a
specialisation, their fees should reflect the increased worth to
your clients.

4 **It's work you can do but don't like to do.** You have
clients you appreciate and respect, clients who are important
to you, and you don't wish them to leave in preference for
another professional. When they ask you to do work that is
within your area of competency but is not enjoyable, charge
more for it. Some clients rightfully demand that I go on
site to consult with their people as the cost and logistics of
doing it the other way are prohibitive and unwieldy. There
are some places I don't like to travel, so I've developed a
tiered fee structure that recompenses me (and my family) for
inconvenient and overlong travel. The client appreciates that
the value of my contribution greatly exceeds my fees, and
I'm more comfortable making the additional effort when
being paid exceptionally well. You are within your rights and
it is entirely appropriate for you to charge higher fees for
work that is unenjoyable or inconvenient.

5 **The work is challenging and requires you to acquire new skills.** As clients assimilate with you and come to depend on you, there will be times where they seek your assistance in areas that will necessitate the acquisition of new knowledge or skills. You may need to learn, or to acquire additional resources that already have the skills (this could be in the form of a new employee or the engagement of a subcontractor). For example, the CEO of a mining and resources company engaged my services to deliver educational programs to middle management on change management, systems thinking and 6 Sigma. My areas of expertise do not include 6 Sigma so I engaged the services of an internationally recognised consultant. My fee not only reflected my contribution, but included all of the costs for the subcontracting consultant and additional recompense to me for managing the entire project.

6 **Acceding to unusual requests.** Sometimes unusual projects present themselves and your contribution places particular challenges on you. I received a request to speak at a conference where the audience were private bankers to high-net-worth individuals in the United Arab Emirates. Prior to confirming the engagement there was a teleconference involving the CEO, four members of the board and me to discuss the details and arrangements. During the conversation the CEO exclaimed how valuable it would be if his private bankers could get access to me for private one-on-one meetings, where I could address their specific individual issues. 'Ric, do you have any ideas on how to make this work?' There were far too many bankers for me to have meetings with all of them, and why would I be so presumptuous as to think they would all want to spend time with me anyway. I suggested that I 'set up shop' in the foyer directly outside the conference room for the two-day conference and make myself freely available to any of his people to sit with me and share a 20-minute coffee. The fee charged was substantially more than the normal two-day consulting contract. Value trumps price.

7   **You are the chosen expert for blue–chip companies.**
References, as a marketing tool, seem to be relegated to
testimonials on a website or, worse, the ubiquitous 'client
list' hidden somewhere in the murky depths of that same
website. If you have attracted the patronage of immediately
recognisable blue–chip (Fortune 500) companies, it's
incumbent on you to let your marketplace know how highly
regarded you are by the best companies in the land. If this
sounds a trifle boastful then you need to boost your self-
esteem, and there's no better way than by boosting your
fees. Significant buyers appreciate the value of dealing with
the best. After all, your role as a professional practitioner is
to improve client results, and if the best companies in the
land are engaging you, then it is obvious that you must be
producing what's required.

Fees are a reflection of your value as perceived by the client (see
figure 10.2). Your perceived value is enhanced by the amount and
quality of interaction and penetration generated by your Whirlpool
Marketing. The better interactions you have via branding,
networking, alliances and so on, the greater your perceived value
in the marketplace.

Figure 10.2: fees reflect perceived value

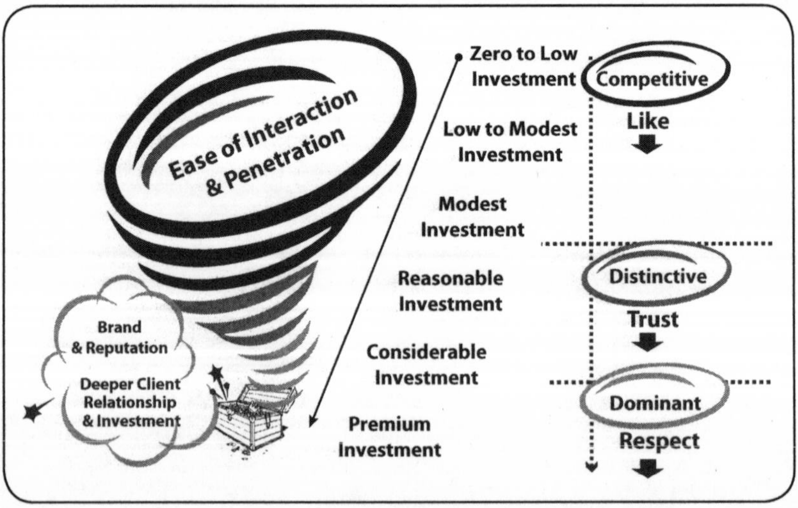

Whirlpool Wisdom

- I don't want to be treated the same as everybody else.

- I'm willing to pay for quality.

- I'm willing to pay for prompt delivery.

- I'm willing to be good-mannered, good-natured and good-humoured, so long as I'm being shown respect, courtesy and honesty.

- I don't want to be treated the same as the person who doesn't want to pay what it's worth, who expects everything for nothing, who affords no loyalty, word-of-mouth or repeat business.

- I'm your A-class client and I demand that you treat me differently from those clients who are not.

It's a myth that everyone should be treated equally, especially in your business.

Negotiate lower fees, when appropriate, without losing credibility

Don't be so quick to negotiate. That's not to say that you cannot negotiate lower fees, but misjudging the client behaviour as resistance to your fees automatically weakens your position. Many professionals are just too ready to negotiate their fees. Although there are some people who want to negotiate on everything, clients cannot negotiate unless you allow them to. If it's inappropriate (and that's 99.97 per cent of the time), don't negotiate. If there are legitimate and appropriate reasons why you may engage in a negotiation on your fees, then by all means do. However, if you reduce your fees the instant your client takes a breath, or solely because they make an arbitrary comment about the cost, you're just enabling their bad behaviour. Surrendering easily to lowering your fees indicates a lack of self-esteem, and the problem lies at the feet of the professional, not the client. If you don't feel you can negotiate successfully, you won't. If you consider that your value is inadequate compared to the price you're asking, you'll be willing to negotiate a lower fee, quickly. Quite often, simply saying, 'I'm sorry but we never negotiate price' will avert negotiations. But if you have to negotiate on price, there's a problem, at your end. Plain and simple. That problem is almost always the lack of a significant return on investment caused by your not providing clear and significant value to the client. Whenever a prospective client tells you the price is too high, the intrinsic sentiment is that the value is too low. The solution is you must either correct the value you're delivering or better articulate the value in language the client understands.

If you do have to negotiate on price, remove value as you reduce price; that's the quid pro quo. If you lower your price without reducing value, you are simply stating that your fee was too high compared to the value being offered. When prospective clients attempt to bargain your fees, they are taking the attitude that you are a vendor, a sycophant and somehow subservient. You're not a commodity — you are a value proposition. Negotiate positively!

The dentist's model

During the festive season I broke two teeth. Unsurprisingly, I found it impossible to secure a dentist during the Christmas break. The first opportunity was 10.00 am on Friday, January 13. I'm not a triskaidekaphobic, but it did seem ominous. Arriving for my appointment, I sit in the waiting room. A few feet away is a door, behind which lurks a bloodthirsty madman waiting to get his hands on me. From behind this door emanate discomforting muffled noises. To allay my anxiety I pick up a magazine and read the latest gossip: Will Charles wed Diana? (Dentists spare no expense on waiting-room accoutrements.) At 10.35 the dentist calls me into his chamber of horrors. A happy little white-clad nurse sits me in a chair that is NASA surplus from the 2006 Space Shuttle missions. She ties a bib around my neck, which states pretty clearly I am going to bleed — you know you're not there to eat lobster. She presses a button and I am tipped back into a supine and vulnerable position. The dentist walks to a cabinet, removes a drawer of surgical instruments ... and empties them into my mouth — the whole drawer. With my mouth full of sterilised stainless steel, he now asks me all manner of questions. But the dentist seems to understand my grunts, as he studied open-mouth-speak at university.

He delivers the prognosis: 'Ric, I need to make an extraction. Would you like novocaine?'

'YES I want novocaine!' Of course, I'm forgetting the pain this itself involves. You know how it's administered, don't you? A needle is pushed through the roof of your mouth and out the top of your head!

The rest is a blur, until I get the invoice. 'How do you wish to pay for this, Mr Willmot?' My jaws drops wider than when he pulled the tooth. Nobody carries around that sort of cash. I hand over the titanium card.

If you ran your practice on the dentist's model, how long before you would go broke? It's difficult to get to see him, he's late for the appointment, you're made to feel vulnerable, he doesn't really listen to what you say, casually inflicts pain and then charges a princely sum. Why do dentists not only survive but thrive? Because they focus on the value, as the client perceives it. They do nothing else except improve the client's condition. They take away the pain of a broken tooth, improve the smile with teeth whitening, prevent further problems by filling the cavities.

Consider how most other businesses react to increased competition and difficult economic conditions. Bargaining away profitability in the hope of not losing the sale. 'I can do it for less money, I can do it in less time, I can add this for free,' and before you know it they're washing their clients' windows. Businesses are focusing on the negative, on the objections and impediments causing clients to deny the sales. What does the dentist do? He focuses on the value. Will you continue to hear objections when you focus your prospect's attention on the value you have to offer? Certainly, but don't focus there first.

Regardless of what stage your career is at, you should consider these questions:

- Who are your top three new business prospects? How will you move things along with them, quickly and successfully?

- Who are your top three repeat business prospects? How will you encourage that business to continue, promptly?

- What did you learn from the three most recent client acquisitions? How can you leverage that success? How will you use this to improve future acquisitions?

- What did you learn from the three most recent pieces of business you failed to acquire? How can you improve your client acquisition performance based on what you learned?

- Are you fuelling your Marketing Whirlpool and enabling prospective clients to learn about you and your services? Are you doing this in a way that makes it easy for them?

- What Whirlpool Marketing activities can you implement that you haven't yet?

There's never been a better time to start than now!

Discounting

A standard maxim is that professional and personal services practitioners should not negotiate their fees. I've been hearing this now since 1985. Interestingly, what I hear is very different from what I see. 'We don't discount our fees, Ric.' Never? 'No.' What were your write-downs for the past quarter? 'Oh, that's different though, Ric. Write-downs are not discounts.' But of course, they are. Who do you think you're kidding? Accountants and lawyers are shockers at this, and they know it. Net fees that you get to keep are all that matters. You don't get to keep the revenues that form part of your write-downs and you don't get to keep the revenues you discount from the gross amount of fees originally quoted. It's a dangerous practice to discount fees or readily agree to write-downs. The practice can decimate your bankable fees and bring undue pressure on you and your staff to achieve budgets and maintain profit margins.

Websites are propagating at a rapid pace, offering discounts, coupons, sales and wholesale direct. The downside is that this type of business model builds zero loyalty and is balanced on the knife-edge of bankruptcy. There will always be another player who comes into your market space making the same stupid price offers. And some of them will most definitely have deeper pockets than you. What's more, the buying public become accustomed to sales patterns, and for non-essential items—that is, nearly all of the products offered this way—they're willing to wait for the sale. Discounters have no differentiation from their competition other than price, so the consumer merely does an internet search for the same item to compare the prices offered by other websites and stores. And the discounters are now effectively doing the marketing for their competitors. It just doesn't make sense. Right about now you're thinking, what does this have to do with professional services? Well, get ready, because it's coming. This business model, thanks to the ease of internet and outsourcing, is soon coming to a profession near you. Bookkeeping, conveyance work, tax accounting, insurance and superannuation (already here), business services, estate planning...the list goes on.

Those most at risk are generalist, mainstream and mid-tier practices. For those of us who are not in commoditised retail products it's imperative to provide value, build solid customer relationships and nurture loyalty. Quality trumps price for a discerning buyer seeking unique, innovative or specialised advice. The wise will acknowledge that positioning of their practice will be key over the next 10 years.

Deeper into discounting

In an attempt to boost revenues, many businesses have tried to reduce costs through re-engineering, outsourcing, downsizing and the like. Pricing is an undiscovered weapon in the quest for higher revenues. Significant profit upside remains untapped in the pricing area. Addressing your pricing strategy is, in principle, much more attractive than downsizing. There are no severance costs, and no people or organisational issues; and a quick win flows straight through to the bottom line. Table 10.2 (overleaf) shows the amount by which your gross revenues would have to decline following a price increase before your gross profit falls below its present level. For example, at the same 45 per cent margin a 10 per cent increase in price could sustain an 18 per cent reduction in gross revenues.

Table 10.2: price increase comparison

	If your present margin is (%)								
	20	25	30	35	40	45	50	55	60
Your sales could decline by the amount shown below before your gross profit is reduced (%):									
Price increase									
2	9	7	6	5	5	4	4	4	3
4	17	14	12	10	9	8	7	7	6
6	23	19	17	15	13	12	11	10	9
8	29	24	21	19	17	15	14	13	12
10	33	29	25	22	20	18	17	15	14
12	38	32	29	26	23	21	19	18	17
14	41	36	32	29	26	24	22	20	19
16	44	39	35	31	29	26	24	23	21
18	47	42	38	34	31	29	26	25	23
20	50	44	40	36	33	31	29	27	25
25	56	50	45	42	38	36	33	31	29
30	60	55	50	46	43	40	38	35	33

If you are operating your practice with a margin of 45 per cent and you decide to raise prices by 10 per cent, then you could lose 18 per cent of your business volume and still be no worse off. If you don't lose 18 per cent—you're in front! I'm not suggesting you arbitrarily increase your fees by 10 per cent. I do encourage you, however, to reassess the value of your services. Are you positioning your business offerings in the marketplace at their true value to the customer?

Often you will see businesses attempting to gain market share by discounting prices. This is abhorrent to a *value-based* thinker like me. The belief is: 'Get increased market share, or enter the market by charging lower prices.' Rubbish! You're making less profit (if any profit at all) that way, plus the client will expect you to keep your prices low, and you'll end up going broke. Table 10.3 indicates the increase in sales required to compensate for a price discounting policy. For example, if your margin is 45 per cent and you reduce prices by only 10 per cent, you need sales volume to increase by 29 per cent to maintain your profit. Rarely has such a strategy worked in the past and it is unlikely to work in the future.

Table 10.3: price reduction comparison

If your present margin is (%)									
	20	25	30	35	40	45	50	55	60
To produce the same profit your sales volume must increase by (%):									
Price reduction									
2	11	9	7	6	5	5	4	4	3
4	25	19	15	13	11	10	9	8	7
6	43	32	25	21	18	15	14	12	11
8	67	47	36	30	25	22	19	17	15
10	100	67	50	40	33	29	25	22	20
12	150	92	67	52	43	36	32	28	25
14	233	127	88	67	54	45	39	34	30
16	400	178	114	84	67	55	47	41	36
18	900	257	150	106	82	67	56	49	43
20		400	200	133	100	80	67	57	50
25			500	250	167	125	100	83	71
30				600	300	200	150	120	100

Another analogy is the '25 per cent sale' or even worse the 'Half-price sale', which can obliterate your profits and reputation with customers. If you're selling a product or productised service, and employ a mark-up of only 40 per cent, a '25 per cent sale' will require sales volume to increase by a staggering 167 per cent just to maintain the same profitability.

You Can't Make This Up

When the Spanish explorer Hernando Cortez landed at Veracruz, he immediately burned his ships. He said to his sailors: 'You can fight or you can die.' Burning his ships removed the third option: ceding ground and sailing back to Spain. Now and then it requires greater creativity to eradicate excuses than it does to come up with the idea. What factors make it harder for you to surrender poor clients so you may achieve your business objectives? How might you stop the excuses?

The big question is: How will you decide on your pricing model? There is no right or wrong approach. Hyundai has carved out a successful pricing model that fits its product quality and sales volume, just as Mercedes has done. Your pricing model options are limited only by your imagination. Choose what works best for your practice. Once you've made your decision, stay true to it. You cannot be the Rolls-Royce of your profession and then discount your fees at the first sign of client resistance.

Educating your people in marketing and pricing need not be a chore, but neither should it be a one-shot wonder. When I was discussing the implementation of Whirlpool Marketing with the principal of a legal firm, she stated that she'd educate each employee in a module of the whirlpool with a six- to eight-week time frame for engagement and take-up by the employee. Far too long! Thirty days for the learning, adoption and implementation of any whirlpool module is more than enough. You employ your staff for their smarts; allow them to prove it by bringing a reasonable level of intensity to what they do.

CHAPTER 11

The internet, technology and social media

Our actions are like ships which we may watch set out to sea,
and not know when or with what cargo they will return to port.
Iris Murdoch, *The Bell*

There was a time when your parents would introduce you to their accountant when you got your first job and needed to lodge an income tax return. When you married, your parents would introduce you to their bank manager so you could get a home loan. There were no price comparisons, no seeking special deals or options … there was no real negotiation. Not any longer. We've changed, and these decisions are generally made independently, even if we do ask for others' opinion. Much of this opinion is now drawn from social media; like it or not, we'd better get used to this and learn to work with it.

In this chapter you will learn how to maximise your:

- website, a sales rep that never sleeps

- business blog for visibility, repute and value

- social media, as a follower, not a leader.

This is a complicated world and technology has compounded, confounded and contributed to the confusion. Extrapolating technology out further we begin to trudge in the dark amorphous goo of social media. While we, as professionals, must embrace the advance of technology into almost every aspect of our business, we will be most successful if we acknowledge that the human touch has therefore become even more important. It's apparent that services professionals can gain brand awareness from social media and the internet, but most of us appreciate that we do business at an interpersonal level. Communication is key. Texting, tweeting, Facebooking and linking is *not* communication. Pick up the telephone and have a genuine conversation with your clients. Visit them at their premises and take them out for coffee.

Consider how much more you may receive in referrals, recommendations and word-of-mouth if you telephone one client every day to ask them how they are going. Not selling, not promoting your business, not floating another offer, just speaking with them, as you would a colleague or friend. One five-minute telephone call with one client each day is a 25- to 30-minute investment per week. You probably spend more time than that following social media that has nothing to do with growing your business. Consider how much more you may receive in referrals, recommendations and word-of-mouth if you have coffee two or three times a week with clients. Having a 15-minute coffee with three clients cost you 45 to 60 minutes, and no more than $25, per week. That's a very affordable investment in your business marketing. You are likely spending more time than that reading email jokes and visiting websites that have nothing to do with growing your business. And most of us already spend about that much on coffee for ourselves anyway.

Viral marketing through social media may be valuable to Carlsberg Beer and Benetton condoms, but professional services marketing is different. It's not a product. It's not a commodity, and it's not sold through social media. Buyers want a competent expert, not a gimmicky salesperson. Professional services advice is, as the name indicates, a professional service.

A warning: Don't get cutesy with your online marketing. Don't do it. It's silly and hurts you more than it helps you. I received a marketing email in which the writer apologised that the link didn't work in a piece sent the previous day. I'd been receiving increasing numbers of emails from this person and this one got me thinking. I checked the previous message, which was still in my trash folder, clicked the link and ... it worked! The second email with 'the correct link' was sent solely—and in my opinion, manipulatively—to attract attention to their marketing. I've unsubscribed. This type of online marketing is annoying and futile. Market smarter. Substance and value will always trump volume and mass.

Social media, like other traditional forms of advertising, is a follower not a leader. Sunday afternoon lazing about in the lounge room watching television after partaking of Mum's famous family roast and trifle dessert guarantees that no matter how much fast food advertising you are exposed to during the commercials you will not be inclined to cruise through the drive-through. All of that advertising is wasted on you. However, if you haven't eaten during the day and arrive home to an understocked refrigerator, an advertisement may be all the prompt you need to choose fast food as tonight's dining solution. The advertising did not lead you to make a purchase, but it influenced your decision after you established a desire to eat with the limited choices available at that moment.

Social media is also a follower and not a leader in the context of marketing professional services. Social media, including blogs and websites, may provide supporting collateral for buyers considering your services who think to research you, your firm and your reputation online. So having a credible online presence can support your sales and marketing efforts, but it will rarely create sales opportunities in and of itself. Some of the ways the internet and social media can support your marketing efforts are:

- building a repository of worthwhile intellectual property, tools and diagnostics

- broadcasting announcements of interest to your potential buyers

- creating an image of you and your business that supports your mainstream marketing message

- efficiently sharing video, audio and other large files that you're willing to be publicly and freely consumed (another form of testimonial)

- supporting other mainstream advertising or marketing efforts

- developing brand awareness.

Gone are the days when your website was a static electronic brochure for your practice. It is now a marketing and prospecting tool to attract new customers. Just as people don't drive the freeways to look at advertising billboards, they don't trawl the internet looking to be sold something. People need a compelling reason to visit your website. Your site must be a valuable resource. It must in some way be helpful and useful to visitors, and information found there must be usable — for example:

- articles, case studies, position papers, white papers, research papers and research results

- audio and video recordings., diagnostics, ready reckoners and other business tools

- links to other useful websites that are relevant to your visitors.

Your website should portray the strengths of your firm and the results clients can expect to achieve from engaging you. It promotes you and strengthens your reputation and brand — it's a sales representative for your firm that never sleeps. Your goal is to have potential customers experience you, your offerings and your expertise. They should be able to find out more about you and your people, how you do things and why you're genuinely different from the competition. If it is designed and maintained correctly, the website will build your credibility. It is not just for today but forever, and content is key. It should be a storehouse of continually updated and improved information and advice to inspire and educate.

It's a common question: Why should your professional practice have a blog when everyone is now doing it? The purpose of a blog is to attract clients and grow your business. It's not to share photographs of your pets or Aunt Mable losing her false teeth as she snores in the sun-chair. A blog may help your business:

- become known and create visibility with your target audience

- build your brand, repute and authority

- create referrals

- improve search engine visibility

- create value for your clients and potential market

- improve longevity

- generate business inquiry.

Some internet marketing gurus will tell you that you *must* have a blog. Not true. You must decide if it makes sense for you and your firm. So what do you need to know about business blogging?

- Who will be reading the blog? Who do you want to read the blog?

- Why do you want these people reading your blog? What's your objective?

- What do the readers want and need that you can provide in your blog?

- What stories do you have to share? Why you and not your competitors? Why are you more valuable?

Three assets a business blog can bring to your organisation are visibility, repute and value. To make business blogging worthwhile for your professional practice, you must be disciplined to regularly post articles in a consistent way. People will soon lose interest if they never know when you might next post an update. Here's my pragmatic, non-technical advice to you regarding a business blog:

- Create categories to make it easy for visitors to find what they want.

- Always deliver content that is compelling, relevant and, where possible, remarkable. Monitor comments and delete spam or vulgarity. Be genuine, approachable, helpful and friendly.

- Interact with your readers to create greater engagement. When people make the effort to leave comments on your blog, take the time to respond to them. All of them! This ensures they feel appreciated for being involved with your media.

- Vary the length of your posts. Treatises are not very popular with blog readers, however. Best to keep the majority of posts concise and pithy. Provide overwhelming value.

- Promote your practice now and then — it's allowable and probably a good idea.

- Use a well-known and easily managed blog platform.

- Make the blog visually and intellectually attractive. Have it professionally designed — you don't want it looking like you did it yourself, unless of course that's your profession.

- Make your blog interesting by incorporating articles, polls, surveys, case studies, white papers, video and audio.

- Add a new article or post at least once a week.

Whirlpool Wisdom

The truth in business is that you cannot please everyone. Some people won't like your options. Some won't like your price or your timing. Some won't like your methodology, your terms or your payment options. There will always be someone who can find fault with something about your business. Determine what your business model is, and how that model is best suited to the types of clients you specifically want. Then stay true to it. Proudly exclude those that don't fit. It's in their best interest, and yours.

'Build it and they will come.' Not so, when you're referring to the internet and social media. You must proactively promote your blog if it is to produce any results for your practice. You must drive people to your media. Ways to promote your blog include:

- promoting through replicating posts on LinkedIn

- article marketing in mainstream media

- promoting blog posts via Twitter and Facebook alerts

- guest posting on other blogs followed by your potential clients

- link building and SEO

- promoting in your hard-copy marketing collateral

- promoting in the signature file of all employees' emails

- promoting by linking with your website

- raising it in conversation if appropriate. ('I've provided a few alternatives on how to handle that very issue in my blog. You should check it out, and bookmark it so you can refer to it when you need those answers again in the future.')

You must provide genuine value to convert one-time visitors into subscribers, customers and advocates. To do this you must appeal to *their* interests, not yours. What content do you utilise to convert visitors into customers and advocates? Educate your readers and help them and their businesses to get better. This is achieved by informing your readers through your content, showing them how to solve the problems most likely confronting them. Demonstrate how your solutions work and the results that can be achieved by following your advice. You are free to promote your service offerings — it's your blog — but any offers you make must match readers' wants and needs. When you are consistently reaching the last two points on the conversion curve (see figure 11.1), you're being successful and the blog has been worth the effort.

Figure 11.1: the blog conversion curve

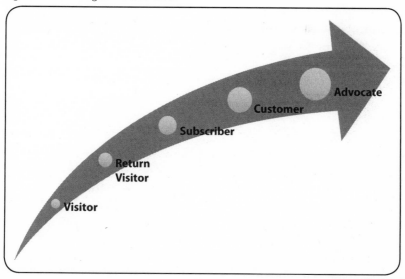

The currency to move visitors along the conversion curve to 'client' and 'advocate' is to provide opportunities for them to sample your offerings. You can encourage sampling by offering ways for your visitors to taste test your intellectual property. The sampling you offer should be of such immense and positive value that they want more. This will also lead to positive word-of-mouth. Positive experiences encourage people to share what they've discovered, and these shared experiences create a powerful trust in your brand. Blogging is not a popularity contest. You are much better served by having 100 interested readers who will do business with you than 10000 readers who will never invest a cent with you but love what you've got to say.

> ## Ric's Tip
>
> Enterprises are paid to create transferable value, not simply to be popular.

Have a professional integrate your other social media such as Twitter, Facebook and LinkedIn with your blog. This way, you only have to make one article post to your blog and that article is automatically posted to your other social media platforms. This improves your efficiency and minimises time spent on such activities. Blogging does seem like a natural and effective instrument for anyone in professional services. It is easy to implement and inexpensive to get started, and it's a good channel through which to share your opinions, ideas, perspectives and solutions on key issues. But before you launch, be certain you're willing and able to commit to this marketing activity. You must keep the blog active, fresh, interesting and effective. This is the only way you can guarantee to attract and retain your targeted readers, and maintain their interest. Consider your blog as part of your 'give to get'. Blogging needs to be diverse, interesting, fun, easy to read, and appealing to both logic and emotion. Outsource whatever you can to minimise your time and effort. Consider if the blog is replacing some other marketing effort or is run in conjunction with existing efforts. Allocate human as well as organisational and financial resources. If you are going to do this, do it properly. Remember, the blog is out there for everyone to see; it represents you and your practice just as your reception area, letterhead and business cards do. Ensure that it is well organised and easy to navigate. Your blog is there to serve.

From the Front Lines

'In the '90s I was a product manager for a large telecommunications company. One of my product manager co-workers was in charge of a direct mail campaign promoting a new overseas calling product. After months of copy and design changes, and layers of legal approvals and sign-offs, the mailing piece was finally approved. 300 000 promotional pieces were printed ready to hand over to the mailing house for distribution. My product manager co-worker got a few samples from the printing company and showed them off proudly. His boss picked up one of the pieces, looked at it and his face drained of colour. The call-to-action telephone number was wrong. It was a dummy number (1800 555 555) used for layout purposes during the design process. That dummy number was never changed to the genuine campaign telephone number before printing. So 300 000 mailing pieces had to be pulped. The good news was they had not been mailed before the error was spotted. The lesson learned: if you are in charge of a marketing campaign, make sure you personally call every number, visit every website and test every email address before pushing the print button. And now with the addition of social media, there are even more chances for things to go wrong. Measure thrice, tweet once.'

—John Hacking, Product Manager, Search Tempo

The big question for many professionals is: What should I write about on my blog? The articles on your blog have to be good. They have to be relevant and worthwhile to the reader. If you want to be noticed, I suggest you try a controversial and provocative style of writing. It has worked well for me over the years. For a number of years in Australia I was known as 'The Contrarian Consultant'. (I consciously moved away from that brand when so many other 'contrarians' appeared on the consulting landscape.) As an example, no one needs the seven–millionth blog post about why leaders need followers. Never worry about or judge yourself by the number of hits, page views, external reviews and critiques, or unsolicited responses criticising your work. Do make sure, however, that your posts support your practice's fundamental value proposition.

Give yourself permission and be willing to close the blog and walk away if you are not posting regularly or you determine it is not producing a suitable result for the time and effort being invested. Your blog content should be derived from the 'sweet spot' in figure 11.2.

Figure 11.2: the blog content sweet spot

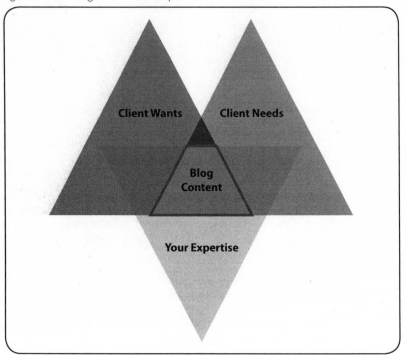

As with any facet of your business, creating a process can assist in getting it done successfully, as intended. Create an editorial calendar to stimulate your thinking and help you plan, prepare, research and keep to schedule. Systematising your blog makes it easier and less intrusive on your time. You can and should share responsibility throughout your practice so the blog content doesn't weigh on just one person. The branding of your blog does not have to match that of your website exactly (that could prove confusing), but it should be consistent and complementary to your website and other marketing collateral.

The bottom line in all of this is that you enjoy writing and you are reasonably competent at the craft. Spelling and grammatical mistakes will not present the image and sophistication required to support your assertion of being a quality thought leader in a professional services sector.

Best Practices

If you are going to involve yourself in social media, then make yourself the centre of a whirlpool in which people are attracted to you and your smarts. Start your own group on LinkedIn where you call the shots and control the discussion. This will allow you to make your ideas, strategies and collateral available to the members of the group, who may become future clients because they have been exposed to your intellectual property.

The ultimate abyss of a professional's time is social media. Like black holes in space, social media are the dark monsters of technology that eat everything that wanders too close—dense objects with extremely high gravity that trek cyberspace preying on the unwitting. Be aware of their existence, respect that they have a place in the universe, and keep your distance. Unless your profession is technology, have someone else handle the internet and social media on your behalf. Seek out and engage a technology professional who can project manage your website, blog and other social media and leave it to them. Don't do it yourself. There are far better uses of your time that can produce a substantial return on investment. And there are outstanding technology consultants who can proactively suggest ideas, concepts and tactics to support the strategy of your practice consistent with your fundamental value proposition.

You Can't Make This Up

There were purportedly 20028351 LinkedIn connections to me as of 3 January 2014; 1980 of those are direct connections that I genuinely know in one way or another. The others...well, I have no idea! Added to this I have a few thousand followers on Twitter, but I myself do not follow anyone. Without fail, at least once every two or three months I will receive an irate email berating my failure to observe Twitter etiquette. This person, whom I have never met, and with whom I have never previously corresponded, chooses to follow me and declares that I am expected to reciprocate. Never mind that my profile—which one has to view in order to follow me—makes it clear that I have a few thousand followers and I'm not following anyone; so why would I make an exception for this one person? If this is the level of intellect to be found on social media, I'm okay with not participating.

Determine what you expect to achieve in implementing a website presence and social media platform. Remember that this type of branding and advertising will rarely generate new business opportunities or leads in and of itself. It will be a follower, not a leader. For instance, I am active on LinkedIn because it has such great acceptance within the business community and there is a plethora of subgroups that focus on specific areas. Being a member of these groups allows you to share your intellectual property and other members to share your articles with their contacts. Potential buyers of your services may become aware of your expertise through regular exposure to your intellectual property shared through platforms such as this. If and when they have a need, or by serendipity you have personal contact with them, your credibility is supported by this previous exposure. Engaging a competent technology professional and automating the dissemination of your intellectual property reduces the time you need to invest personally. Here is an example: my *Weekly Wisdom* newsletter (ISSN 1837-8552) is disseminated through mail client software. The software automatically posts the newsletter to my Twitter account, Facebook page and LinkedIn without any human engagement. This is incredibly efficient.

Strive to make engaging and interacting with you through technology, the internet and social media as easy as possible for the people you're attempting to reach. Contrary to the advice of many, be willing to allow people to download your audio, video and case studies without requiring them to enter personal contact details such as an email address. If you want people to have your intellectual property, give it to them without driving them away by asking for information that may cause them to fear they will become the recipient of an ongoing email bombardment. If you are unwilling to give away your intellectual property to anyone who wants it, then perhaps you should consider productising it and placing it on your website for sale, say as a downloadable e-book. Make up your mind which it is to be, and then get comfortable with your decision.

The pundits of the internet, technology and social media tell you to focus on the hits. How many website visitors do you have each month? How many page views do you receive on your blog? How many likes are you getting on Facebook? How many retweets? I don't care one iota. In professional services it takes only one quality hit to give you your next $50 000 project or client. Success is not measured by hits, views or likes. It is measured by adding clients engaged, revenues invoiced and profits banked.

Pragmatism is your ally. Remain conservative with your expectations of what social media can do for your professional practice in generating new revenues. As you implement your strategy incorporating your online presence consider what your ideal clients will be most receptive to, and how much time will transpire between your marketing activity and the prospective client action. I've yet to hear one of my clients tell me they won a new piece of business solely because of a 140-character tweet. Rational and prudent thinking about how much money, time and resources you will invest in your social media is more appropriate than overexcited optimism fuelled by the technology gurus.

Continually measure the results of all facets of your online marketing, and determine what is proving useful to your business results. You can then make informed decisions on what you can exploit and receive a return on investment from, what you might need to adapt to improve results, and what you should abandon completely. Treat technology as you would any other piece of infrastructure or business capital in your organisation: evaluate the cost, estimate the returns, measure the actual returns and evaluate the viability of its continuance. You would not employ a new staff member without reading her résumé and interviewing her for the role. You would also have a probationary period during which you can choose to opt out of the engagement. There would be ongoing evaluation and measurement against expected performance and outcomes. For most of us, social media and the internet are still magical and incompletely understood, but this does not mean they should not be held accountable to the same level of scrutiny as a staff member or high-end colour photocopier machine.

Social media and technology will continue to be integrated ever more deeply into the marketing of our professional practices. Determine exactly what you expect from its involvement in your business, the objectives it is to achieve and the benefits your firm will derive. By working backwards you can now ascertain what technology you need to introduce, how it is to be implemented and who is going to project manage the resource. Benchmarks, deadlines and minimum expectations can be set. If all the targets are achieved you can happily continue. If not, reassess, adapt or abandon.

Advocates of social media will cite research indicating that large percentages of business managers and executives use the internet to gain information. Unfortunately, this has led some people to conclude that social media will help professional services firms gain new business, which is entirely untrue. The CEO of Coca-Cola doesn't trawl the internet looking for a new lawyer or accountant or consultant. And be warned: before anyone cites a single instance that contradicts the truth of this, understand that the exception does not make the rule.

During a conference speech I lament that some technology designed to assist our productivity is actually hindering our effectiveness to do smart business. I explain that while clients attempting to arrange a meeting with me will be tapping away for minutes on their Boysenberries and Sungsams searching for the calendar functions, the yearly planner of my Filofax is open and at the ready, instantly. Afterwards, an individual approaches me and, showing no manners, interrupts a private conversation. Holding her business card in the tips of her fingers, she waves it in my face saying, 'You need to learn how to use your technology better to improve your business. I can teach you.'

I'm no longer interested in her business card even as she thrusts it into my palm. My conversation partner chortles as I tear up the card and discard it. Nesbitt was correct when he wrote, 'high tech … high touch'. The more technology becomes a part of our lives, the more we need to reach out and touch people to build positive, caring and worthwhile relationships. Interrupting a private conversation to tell me my business needs improving is not going to help you build a relationship with me. It's one thing to embrace technology and social media to draw upon the advantages they can bring to marketing your practice. It's quite another to be so infatuated as to think they alone can win you new business.

This entire disquisition on the marketing of professional services finally leads me to the point of Whirlpool Marketing: by devoting as little as 20–40 minutes a day to engaging in regular and consistent marketing activities that are applied to support a purposeful strategy, a need is created for you and your services that:

- is not a commodity and is not fulfillable by just professional offerings

- positions you as of intrinsically higher value for the buyer

- hits upon emotional influence, not just logical understanding

- is results-oriented, not input-oriented (like most other marketing approaches)

- increases urgency and action by the client to engage with you

- bestows high credibility in you and your expertise, enabling you to create partnerships with your clients

- affords you the advantage of circumventing the competition.

Create an action sheet that outlines what marketing activity you will undertake each day to share your smarts with the key buyers of your offerings. Then they will come knocking on your door asking how you may help them.

Sports contests are won at the close, not the start. Basketball, football, golf, cricket... games can be won or lost in the closing minute or the final play. Winning requires preparation, strategy, skill, coaching, toughness, fitness and the right mental attitude. To be the best you have to be disciplined, focused and able to perform under pressure. Professional services is exactly the same. Many professionals who cannot or will not market intelligently drift aimlessly, pushed around by wind and tide on oceans procellous, arriving at ports where they never planned to go. The Marketing Whirlpool is the best asset for your practice, because it allows you to navigate turbulent waters and sail to the destination of your choosing.

Appendix: Tools and resources

Examples of how professional practices usually measure business performance

1   Gross revenues

2   Total operating profit

3   Growth in gross income

4   Profit as a percentage of gross income

5   Salaries as a percentage of gross income

6   Revenue per employee

7   Overhead as a percentage of direct expenses

8   Working capital as a percentage of average monthly operating expenses

9   Ratio of current assets to current liabilities

10 Average ageing for Accounts Receivable

Examples of how professional practices implement Whirlpool Marketing to grow business performance

1   Number of presentations made to professional and trade associations

2   Number of articles published in mainstream media

3   Number of articles published in professional and trade magazines

4   Number of prospective clients declined following Client Assessment Profile analysis

5   Income derived from the sale or licensing of intellectual property

6   Hours of professional development per employee

7   Number of new clients acquired directly through proactive and passive referrals

8   Growth in revenue from existing clients' purchasing new services

9   Growth in revenue from strategic alliances

10 Net operating enjoyment

Brand differentiation techniques

Publicity and promotion

- Webinars and teleconferences
- Seminars and workshops
- Public speaking and presentations
- Publications and marketing collateral
- Business development research
- Handling of new business enquiries
- Research, surveys and case study development

Technology

- Website and blog
- Premium client access
- Email signature files
- Computers
- Social media (including policies on staff usage)
- Company pages on LinkedIn and Facebook

Services

- Client on-boarding program
- Formalised client review process
- Uniformity of proposals
- Pricing policy
- Uniformity of presentation materials
- Customer service feedback
- Exit interviews for clients

Staffing

- Dress code
- Offices and workstations
- Staff meetings
- Staffroom catering
- Employment contracts
- Job titles and role descriptions
- Employee benefits
- Employee termination policy and procedures
- Information sharing
- Talent management system
- Exit interviews

Administration

- Presentation of premises
- Reception area
- Signage
- Bathrooms
- Meeting rooms and boardroom
- Letterhead and business cards
- Marketing materials and collateral

40 ways to create propulsive power to build momentum in your Marketing Whirlpool

1	Advertising	16	Teleseminars
2	Passive listings	17	Podcasts
3	Networking	18	Videos
4	Referrals	19	Special reports
5	Testimonials	20	Surveys
6	Website	21	Research
7	Newsletters	22	Case studies
8	Articles in others' newsletters	23	Workshops
		24	Public seminars
9	Blog posts	25	Shopping cart
10	Posts on others' blogs	26	Products
11	Articles	27	Passive income
12	Booklets	28	Speaking
13	Books	29	Press releases
14	E-books	30	Quoted in media
15	Webcasts	31	Television

32 Radio

33 Direct mailing

34 Interviews

35 Alliances

36 Affiliates

37 Community association leadership

38 Trade association leadership

39 Word-of-mouth

40 Serendipity

The Trust Whirlpool

Acquiring new business is significantly easier when you are perceived to be a trusted adviser. Building trust is a proactive process, just like any other facet of the Marketing Whirlpool. Here are 17 ways you can add energy to your 'Trust Whirlpool':

1   Publish with third-party endorsement (e.g. publications).

2   Elicit and publicise testimonials.

3   Systematise your Referral Whirlpool.

4   Accept every opportunity to speak when influencers will be in the audience.

5   Do pro bono work in the community.

6   Volunteer for a leadership position on a board or charitable association's committee.

7   Keep your website current, relevant and interactive.

8   Disseminate a regular newsletter.

9   Offer free diagnostics, resources and other instruments on your website.

10 Create your own best practice from the wisdom and experience gained in your profession.

11 Transfer your intellectual capital (intangible) into intellectual property (tangible).

12 Be a guest lecturer at a university, business school or TAFE.

13 Blog frequently on provocative and current issues.

14 Host breakfasts and luncheons for networking and discussion.

15   Maintain a quality office environment (physically and culturally).

16   Maintain quality employee performance and attitudes.

17   Seek professional association leadership roles.

Brainstorming session template for marketing your professional practice

Many professionals who join my Mentor Program have never identified their true positioning in the market to sell their service offering, largely because they never thought they had to sell. They imagined they would hang out a sign on the building and people would flock in to give them their business. Today professional services providers need to stand out from the crowd to attract new business. Completing this diagnostic will help you focus on the true value of your service offering and who will pay you handsomely for that work.

What problems do you solve? What problems do prospective clients have that you can solve? People don't buy tax returns. They buy tax minimisation strategies. People don't buy financial plans. They buy business expansion ideas. They buy ways to create and accumulate wealth.

_____

_____

_____

What makes you the expert? What makes you the best person to do this? How are you the expert? Why should it be you rather than anyone else who does this? People want to know why they should choose you. What makes you, your advice and your results stand out from other professionals in your field?

_____

_____

_____

What marketing collateral supports and demonstrates how you help clients? What marketing collateral do you have supporting and demonstrating your uniqueness and expertise? Do you have published articles, special reports, books, audio programs, videos, web-based learning programs? Are they freely available on your website or blog?

_____

_____

_____

What differentiates you from your competitors who offer similar expertise? What is it about you that will cause clients to engage you rather than your competitors? When you answer this question, read your response aloud and ask: 'So what?' If you're unable to articulate a compelling response … rethink your answer.

_____

_____

_____

Who wants you, specifically? Who in particular wants you and the service you offer? Not everybody is, nor should they be, a prospect for you. Focus on where and how to market yourself and your services efficiently and effectively to the right clients.

_____

_____

_____

Why and how is your point of difference valuable? Why and how is your point of difference valuable to a client? What do they get because of it?

_____

_____

_____

How will the client change because they engaged you?
How is the client better today because they hired you yesterday?
What do you bring to the client (in the form of outcomes and
results) that makes them and their business better?

_____

_____

_____

How can the client measure the value? How can the client
determine if they are making a wise investment? What metrics or
value units can you offer that will demonstrate to the client they
are spending their money wisely by hiring you?

_____

_____

_____

Whirlpool triage

Stage I: Commencing the activity that builds a Marketing
Whirlpool. Slow to begin, not expecting results or a return on
investment. Realising that until this is in place, there is no attraction
or ability to generate a centrifugal force of acquisition.

Stage II: Movement and motion is obvious, and there is a clear
indication that there is depth and power building.

Stage III: A powerful vortex is generating ongoing attraction and
acquisition that feeds existing and future power and growth.

Special thanks

Professional Services Marketing Wisdom was originally conceived thanks to the cajoling and urging of some very special people. Ralph Waldo Emerson said, 'Nothing great was ever achieved without enthusiasm.' A number of these people were so enthusiastic about the Whirlpool Marketing concept that they threw their full support behind making it happen long before Wiley offered me a contract. I'd like to formally thank them, and publicly acknowledge who they are.

Sean O'Donnell, Managing Director at Mindbank Australia

David Smith, Managing Director at DAME Consulting

Brent Szalay, Managing Partner at Seiva Accountants

John Nicolas, Partner at Gaden's Lawyers

Tatiana Porter, Partner at Haycroft Workplace Solutions

Anthony Nicholls, Managing Partner at HNA Accountants

Jesse Yvanoff, Principal at CJ Advisory

Peter Duffy, Partner at Wilson Ryan Grose Lawyers

Meredith Freeman, Principal at Leading Edge Computers

Mark Douglas, Managing Director at Martin Personnel

Adrienne McLean, Principal at The Speakers Practice

Ric Willmot
Managing Director
Executive Wisdom Consulting Group Pty Ltd
PO Box 44
Carina QLD 4152 Australia
Telephone: +61 7 3395-1050
Facsimile: +61 7 3395-1805
Ric@ExecutiveWisdom.com
ExecutiveWisdom.com
RicWillmot.com

Visit our website for:

- a subscription to our free, monthly electronic newsletter, The Executive Wisdom Times (ISSN 2201-5973)

- inclusion on our notification list for new products, workshops and services

- access to over 200 free, indexed articles

- access to a variety of other resources for self-development and professional growth.

Special Offer for Purchasers of This Book

Since the inception of my coaching and mentoring program, more than 240 members from 15 countries have graduated. Some have gone on to sign up again—to become repeat offenders. As a purchaser of this book, you are entitled to a deep discount on membership of the Private Clients Coaching & Mentoring Program. The program offers six months of unlimited access to me for personalised coaching and mentoring by telephone, fax, email and video conferencing. To join this elite group of alumni who have made the professional commitment to dramatically improve their business results, send an email with a scanned copy of your book purchase receipt to: Club@ExecutiveWisdom.com

Index

business revenues
—opportunities to grow 28
—from referrals 148
buyer's psychology 38
buyers response 6

Caltex 83
Cialdini, Robert 38
client assessment profile 190–195
client commitment 34
client engagement 36
client meeting, in social settings
179
client reactivation 125
client relationship 131, 177
—long-term 9–12
—nurturing 133
—provide early value in 90–91
—respond in real time 171
client relationship, keys to
cementing 134–139
—accounting professionals
134–135
—marketing whirlpool
137–138
—sensational customer service
134
client retention 102–104
—customer service and 104
—factors contributing to
103–104
clients
—communication with 156
—educating 142, 148,
151–152
—engaging 167–168
—nexus 100
—passion for nurturing and
understanding 178
—planning for future sales
with 133
—preparation for new 5

—selection of 5–6
—selectively choosing 189
—service pricing and value for
198–199
—testimonial 164
—values 9–13
client's values
—beyond direct fees 12–13
—long-term value, assessment
of 9–12
client testimonial
—formal and informal
94–95
—tangible and intangible value
of 48
commitment to your customers
178
communication 156, 159, 212
see also effective communication
—customers 178
—market 100
competencies and capabilities
—benefits of promoting
132–133
—fees and 199
conversation, control 157–159
customer-centric culture
167–171
—customer experience
enhancement 171
—multiple opportunities for
clients 170
customer-centric perspective,
developing 169
customer interactions
172
customer life cycle 4
customer relationship see client
relationship
customer service 166–167 see also
client relationship
—earning referrals by 132

Learn more with practical advice from our experts

Winning the War for Talent
Mandy Johnson

Web Marketing that Works
Adam Franklin and Toby Jenkins

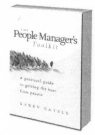

The People Manager's Toolkit
Karen Gately

Start with Hello
Linda Coles

Microdomination
Trevor Young

Digilogue
Anders Sörman-Nilsson

Stop Playing Safe
Margie Warrell

Power Stories
Valerie Khoo

The Ultimate Book of Influence
Chris Helder

Available in print and e-book formats

WILEY

Printed in Australia
02 Jan 2019
694510